C000278652

Thinking Club

I dedicate this book to my mum, Sylvia Lowery, who has worked so hard to help me. From as early as I can remember she has been there.

Thinking Club

A filmstrip of my life as a person with autism

Alex Lowery

Published by Dolman Scott Ltd 2015

Copyright © 2015 Alex Lowery

Photography by Karen Maguire

Book cover design & typeset by Cloud 10 Creative Ltd.

ISBN: 978-1-909204-66-9

Dolman Scott Ltd
www.dolmanscott.co.uk

TABLE OF CONTENTS

FOREWORD

Alex was born on the 12th October 1993, three weeks late. Alex was way past his due date but, when he decided to come, it was rapid and he was nearly born in the car on the way to hospital. From birth Alex had problems: he had weeping eczema and had numerous chest infections, which were treated with steroids and antibiotics. As soon as Alex was able, he would pull his body as far away as possible when he was breastfeeding. Many nights were spent playing the Thomas the Tank Engine videos because this was the only way to stop Alex from screaming. Alex's scream was high pitched and deafening and it was obvious that he was in extreme distress.

When Alex was three I realised his language was delayed and he was having a lot of extreme meltdowns. I took him to the GP and within seven months we found ourselves sat in front of a psychiatrist who told us that Alex had classic autism.

This book has been written by Alex. I have learned so much about autism through the process of Alex writing this book. I have lived through Alex's life, but hearing it from Alex's perspective has filled in a lot of the gaps. I was very distressed when Alex first described how his senses were all mixed up and how all the normal sensations of life such as lights and noise were torture. I was also amazed at how Alex could recall early parts of his life when I would have thought he couldn't understanding what was going on.

Alex began writing this book with Annette Adamson when he was 16. Alex would speak his memories and Annette would write them down.

Alex was only part way through his book when Annette moved away and was no longer able to work with Alex. Annette has still worked on the editing of the book via e-mail. The rest of the book was written either through Alex writing or Alex dictating to me. When Annette had edited a chapter of the book and sent the document back I would read the section out to Alex and he would tell me if he was happy with the changes. There was a lot of sending back and forward. This was a painstakingly slow process. Once this stage of editing was completed the book was read by a number of people and mistakes and suggestions for change were made by a number of people. Alex's Dad, his brother Ben, his sisters Esther and Naomi, and Trudy Kinlock, a family friend, have all helped in this way. Lynn Plimley read through the book and has written a review. Alex's mentor, Margaret Carter of Patchwork Foods, encouraged Alex to include some new chapters on his public speaking. Suzanne Lowery, Alex's sister-in-law, has designed the cover and helped with the formatting. Esther Lowery Alex's sister helped Alex to come up with the chapter headings. I am also very thankful to Karen Maguire who took the photo for the book cover. This book has been a long work in progress and would not be ready to be printed without all the help that has been given. Alex is excited to finally see it in print, and hopes that his story will help others.

Sylvia Lowery
Dee Villa
Holway Road
Holywell
CH8 7NN

CHAPTER 1
The World is a Terrifying Place

My earliest memory is of when I was 3 years old. I was in a world that was a terrifying place, with noises so loud I had to hold my ears to face them. Going into shops is easy for most people, but for me it was one of the worst torments you could have on this earth. The pop music was so loud it was torture. There were so many people walking all around the place it was frightening. I thought the lights that were on the ceiling had pop stars above them on the roof, singing. I was also scared of the dummies that were in the clothes shops – I somehow thought they had something to do with the pop music I could hear. I thought the lights, the pop stars, the music and the dummies were all linked together and they were all evil. I would scream, thinking these 'pop stars' were gods: They were able to be hidden, yet give out a horribly loud noise.[1]

I hated clothes. I only wore loose jogging trousers and t-shirts, but even they felt like I was wearing painfully unbearable armour. The labels felt like needles and the badges on t-shirts felt like thistles sticking into me. Even now I hate to wear a tie; it feels like I'm being strangled slightly. I don't like people to touch me. I feel even a gentle touch will be strange and, when the hand is taken off, I will feel it has left an imprint that is uncomfortable. I also hardly ever feel the cold. When other people say it's cold, I just feel normal. I overreact or underreact to pain. I can bang my head and will yell out loud. Members of my family will come running thinking something terrible has happened. Yet I can cut myself and not notice, and I will often be unaware when my asthma is getting worse. I find people make comments because I haven't reacted to being hit by an object.

In social situations the general noise was too loud. Conversation was confusing to me. What people looked like had a frightening effect. I would be afraid of people if they wore glasses. I would focus on someone's 'long nose' or 'big forehead'; everything was exaggerated. I would find it spooky when people looked at me. People's eyes would look like they were staring at me in an evil way, as if they were some kind of ghost. Ordinary features would become overstated and make people appear creepy. Any background noise would be like a mighty wind. I found all of these things ten times more spine chilling than going to the dentist to get a filling – not that I've ever had that experience, but I think you get the idea.

I found certain types of music horrifying – mostly anything that was loud or sad. So, for instance, anything from pop music to chorales would upset me and make me feel they would bring a great evil upon me. However, I really loved other types of music. In fact, I loved Mozart so much I would shout, "Put Mozart on! Put Mozart on!" I loved the way it made me relax; it was a happy tune, so it didn't worry me. Actually, it seemed to help me.

To add to all of this, I spoke in my own language most of the time. I thought I was speaking like everybody else, but no-one seemed to know what I was saying. I remember feeling so angry because everyone else seemed to understand each other, but no-one seemed to understand me. My mum says I had my own language that I would use as though I was speaking. She says she had begun to tell me that what I was saying didn't make sense. She remembers me screaming when she did this, but it was important for me to know the truth. Until I was nearly 4 my family had humoured me and guessed at what I was trying to say. She says my language did start to come after about a year of me screaming. She also did special work with me, but I did not like it when I found out that others couldn't understand me. Because I was frustrated that no-one could understand me, I would shout "Want my head off!" and scratch myself and pull my own hair. I was confused by the bloodcurdling world around me to which everybody else seemed to belong, but which I couldn't understand. In some ways I still feel like I don't belong to this world. Everyone else seems to be able to understand each other and read other people's body language. I can't do that. I accept this most of the time, but often I wish I could join in more in social settings. I feel frustrated sometimes, but knowing that God loves me helps me to cope. I can feel very angry inside. I don't give in to it because I have been taught that it's wrong to lose control. People have said they think I never get angry, but it's not true.

I was taught about God, but to me He was a frightening idea. I knew God was in church, so I decided that the pastor was God. When I saw the elder, I decided he must be Jesus, because he had a beard. It was a creepy thought: God walking down the aisle, giving communion and preaching! My problem was that I didn't understand anything I couldn't see. My parents were Christians, so I would go to church most Sundays. I didn't go when I was unwell, and apparently I was unwell quite often, but when I did go to church, I remember getting terrified and screaming, "there's gods in there!"

I became afraid of shops and any public building. My mum thinks this fear was triggered by a Halloween display in a shop. That makes sense to me, because when something I don't like happens, I often think it might happen again. Now I can talk and share my fears and worries. Back then I didn't know how, so there was no relief.

Even my home was scary to me. I used to get extremely aggressive and would kick and scream. One day my parents took me to their friend's house. It was quite late and I asked for a drink. I was told, "No, Alex, you're not allowed a drink right now". I lashed out, screaming, thinking they meant I could never have a drink again. My father was cross with me for this outburst, and when we got home I was told off. I became really quiet. I felt terrified. I am told I went on muttering, "Want Mummy! Want Mummy!" It was as though I was lost in my own world. I had no idea why I was in trouble. My dad now says that was the day he definitely knew something was wrong. Just after this, my mum went to a language conference. The speaker actually said that if you tell a child with a language disorder that he can't have a drink now, he thinks you mean never. I must have thought my thirst would never be quenched. My parents still feel guilty about that now.

I was obsessed with Thomas the Tank Engine. I spent hours lining up my die-cast Thomas toys. My favourite teddy was a Thomas toy that ended up with a bent funnel because I carried him everywhere. Although I couldn't have a real conversation, apparently I could recite a lot of the Thomas stories. My older brother, Ben, tells me that he and Naomi (my older sister) would often put on other videos, trying to make them appeal to me by giving them different names! There were one or two films that he actually managed to make me watch in this way, Mary Poppins being one. Ben called it 'Mary pop-star', which is ironic because I hated pop music. I guess as well as being terrified by it, I was also fascinated by it. However, in general, I would only want

Thomas, and would never willingly choose anything else (with the exception of, maybe, the Teletubbies, which I know is bad taste!).

Even when I slept, my world was filled with terror. I had many nightmares. I remember one dream that I had over and over again. It was about Trevor from the Thomas stories, having to be scrapped because he was old and rusty and no-one wanted him anymore. This dream came after watching an episode of Thomas the Tank where Trevor got scrapped. I went to sleep every night worrying about him. My parents say that night after night, I used to shriek while I was asleep. I was in a trance-like state and the only way they could calm me down was to put on the video of Thomas. It wouldn't wake me, but it would pacify me. As soon as the video finished, they say, I would start crying all over again, and this would go on for most of the night. My parents spent night after night without sleep. My dad was even told off in work for falling asleep mid sentence. My parents say they just went into survival mode, and in some ways they can't remember much of this time.

I remember being really excited when I found out that my dad was working with Trevor, wow, I thought, my dad knows Trevor the traction engine. Needless to say he isn't really a traction engine, but it was an exciting idea at the time.

My grandfather used to tell me the story of Little Red Riding Hood. Later, when in bed, I used to dream that I'd turn around and 'see' the wolf lying right next to me. I was petrified! I thought it was real, but my parents didn't know why I was so disturbed because, at the time, I didn't have the language to tell them. Imagine you saw a wolf right next to you in bed, that it was really dark and that you didn't understand about dreams and imaginings; you'd think it was real. You 'see' green eyes staring; sharp teeth bared; jaws opening wide; sharp claws extended, ready to pounce. Horrific, isn't it? Another night, you're going to sleep. It's dark and your bed is right by the window. You look outside. You hear cars in the dark, see headlights shining and you think, 'this is it...the wolf is coming'. I was always looking out of the window at night worried the wolf was on his way. I don't quite know how, but for some reason I thought all the loud cars in the dark meant the wolf was on his way. I can't explain why I thought that, but that's what I thought. I think I thought maybe the wolf is in one of the cars or something.

I was so obsessive that at one point everything had to be blue – even ice cream! My mum says I would yell if I wasn't dressed in blue clothes. I insisted on a blue cup, bowl and spoon. I felt anxious if I didn't get blue things. My mum thinks that, perhaps, the comfort of everything being blue made me feel safer in what was a very fearsome and disjointed world for me. Blue was a colour I knew and liked, mainly, I think, because of Thomas the Tank Engine. I had a blue sleep suit with feet. My mum tells me of the time when she asked a café owner for a blue ice cream. She says the woman looked at her as if she was mad, but my mum was worried about me having another meltdown where I would scream and hurt myself. She says she realized that she had to stop giving into my obsessions all the time. She knew that sometimes she would have to say no and let me have the tantrum. I am thankful that my mum did this, because I think I would be much worse now if she hadn't.

There were certain foods I was obsessive about. I remember choking on food every day. I don't remember much else, but my mum says I used to spit the food out into her hand. She says eventually she helped me to chew by moving my jaw for me with my hand. I hated lots of food, and would only eat things like sausages, which ironically I choked on but still would attempt to eat. Sausages are actually still a favourite of mine, but they're not all I eat.

I was obsessive about clothes too. My mum remembers the time when I insisted on wearing a balaclava and Wellington boots day and night for about four days – I thought I was a Teletubby. Eventually, they took them off me, at which point I would not only scream, but scratch my own face and hurt myself. My mum says she is slightly deaf because my scream was so loud; I used to hit and kick her. I was just so angry because everything hurt me.

It was the day of my 4th birthday when my parents asked, "How old are you?" "3", I said. "No you're not, you're 4", they replied. "I not! I 3!" I said. They said, "No, you're not, you're 4 – it's your birthday today". I said, "If I not 3, I not Alex!" I kicked out – really screaming and hitting myself. It was the thought of being a different age. I thought being 3 years old and being Alex were one and the same thing. I thought if I wasn't 3, then I couldn't be Alex anymore. I thought you stayed at the age you were, which isn't logical, but I didn't understand that then. I hated it when I was told I was a different age to the one I thought I was. I thought everyone had their own name and their own age, which they stayed at forever. I can't quite remember how, but during that day I began to adjust to the idea of being 4 – perhaps it helped that I was given a Thomas cake! All I know is that I didn't have a problem with being a different age ever again (or at least not in the same way) – I might not like the thought of growing up too fast, but at least I haven't been screaming about it!

A little while after this, my mum was expecting my younger sister, Esther. She said, "Look Alex! I've got a baby in my tummy – it's kicking! Can you feel it?" I could feel it and I started to get really excited! My mum often had to go for blood tests to do with this thing called 'ante-natal' (I'm not exactly sure what ante-natal is, but I think it's something that mums go through just before having a baby). When she did, I went with her. As soon as I saw them taking blood from my mum's arm, I screamed, trying to stop them from doing it again. I was really doing everything I could to protect my mum. It was as if they were trying to stab a sword into her rather than just a little needle. I didn't really understand what antenatal was, but I thought 'Aunty Natal' was the name of the nurse who did blood tests. I thought she was evil, and was taking my mum's blood out to be cruel. I knew we often called people 'Uncle' or 'Aunty' so-and-so, so I just thought this nurse was my Aunty – even though I didn't really know what an Aunty was.

Just after Esther was born, I was called into my parent's bedroom, where the baby was laying. "Alex! Come in, the baby's here", my mum called, but when I came in I shouted, "Put baby back! Baby belong in tummy!" They said, "No, Alex, not any more, the baby's been born now". I continued to shout, "No! Baby belong in tummy!" But then Esther whimpered and I said, "Ah, coot!" (Which was my way of saying cute). After that I liked her, and never complained about the baby being out of the tummy ever again. However, there were still problems. I liked to play with her all of the time and, without meaning to, sometimes I would hurt her. One day my mum went downstairs and she found me holding Esther upside down. I also developed a 'baby obsession' – whenever I saw a baby I would run over and try to pick it up, which probably really embarrassed my mum!

My parents say that by this time they had found out that I had a condition called 'autism' (although I didn't know I had it at the time). My mum started doing a little bit of therapy with me, and I did seem to improve because of it. I'm not exactly sure what it was; I think it was sort of improving my social skills and language. In those days I could barely speak, I could say a few words and some small sentences, but I didn't say very much and, in fact, I think that was one of the reasons why I would scream and shout so much – but anyhow, the therapy my mum did certainly helped my language and speaking a little.

After my language had come on a little and I was better at understanding other people, we would go to town so that my mum could help me to develop some safety skills. I had absolutely no concept of road safety or danger. We would stand by the crossing and I'd try to run into the road. My mum would say, "You can't cross the road now Alex, there are too many cars!" However, I thought if you closed your eyes and couldn't see the cars that would mean it was safe. My mum would say, "No, Alex, wait for the green man to come – you can't cross the road until the green man comes." When the green man came, I'd look, but I wouldn't be able to find him. My mum would point and say, "Look, its right in front of you... there!", but I was actually looking for a real-life green man. I was busy looking at all the people, trying to spot the green person! Everything to me was so literal that even the simplest conversations could become filled with misunderstanding!

CHAPTER 2
Disturbed Nights and School

My parents home-educated my older brother and sister, but my parents decided I should go to school. She had just given birth to my sister Esther and I was screaming day and night constantly; my mum was exhausted, and felt she would cope better if she had a break from me during the day.

I have very few memories of my first school, so I'll tell you about my second school – Ysgol Brondyffryn in Denbigh. It was a school where all the children had been diagnosed with Autistic Spectrum Condition. On my first day I don't think I really liked it much. My grandmother has told me that when I first got to the school and saw my classroom with all the other people, I went screaming and shouting to get out. My mum says I sobbed, crying, "Go home! Go home!" As you might have guessed, I was saying I just wanted to go back home.

Although I had improved, I was still having problems. I started off in Class 1 and the teacher was named Mrs Bryer. My parents say Mrs Bryer was a lovely teacher, but I'm afraid I can't remember her very well. The only vivid memory I have of her was that she tried to stop me from stimming (that's short for 'self-stimulating behaviour', which is repetitive behaviour such as hand-flapping, rocking or repeating phrases), which in my case took the form of flapping, squeezing my hands together and rocking back and forth. Apparently I was the worst in the whole school for stimming, literally doing it non-stop. This regardless of how many times Mrs Bryer would try to stop me. I absolutely hated the fact that Mrs Bryer did this. I never managed to stop. I still haven't now, although I don't do it nearly as much as I did back then and I try to control it as much as I can when we are out of the home. It's a battle I haven't won, so I try to manage it, and not get too stressed about stopping it altogether.

Anyway, I did make some friends in the school; I became good friends with a girl and a boy who were in my class. I also became quite good friends with a girl who was on the school bus with me, as well as a few others. There were still problems because, although I had a lot of behavioural problems, there were some students who were much worse than me and would chase me around. Some would bite and scratch (I see now that they weren't meaning to be nasty, they just didn't understand what they were doing), but it scared me and I used to run away because I was so frightened. When I got home I would tell my parents and they'd explain that those children couldn't help it because they had severe difficulties. I really didn't understand it. What did my parents mean? Of course they could help it! I really didn't understand that those children didn't know what they were doing. After all, I didn't even know we all had autism. Sometimes I would complain to the teachers about the children who I thought were being nasty. They'd say, "He's trying to be friendly, he just wants to be your friend".

I suppose I would sometimes get violent too, and scream. According to a file of records which I read about myself, when I wanted to make friends I would go up to a boy in the school randomly and say, "Hello there, boy!" A bit inappropriate to say the least, and not at all guaranteed to win friendship!

There were some parts of the school day that I really liked, such as the food at dinnertime. The cook's name was Manon (I'm not quite sure if I spelt it right), but I loved her food. I'd always say to my mum, "Manon's a good cook; she's a better cook than you!" In fact I would eat food at school that I refused to eat at home.

I enjoyed the singing too. Sometimes they would sing Christian songs – I think by this time I had stopped believing that the Pastor in my church was God and the elder was Jesus. If I'm not mistaken, I still thought the minister was some sort of 'King' guy, and I'm not 100% sure that I still didn't think he was 'God'. Even at this point, I still didn't believe in things that I couldn't see. Maybe I didn't even believe God was real, but who knows? It was all still very confusing. Another song I really liked was one called 'Doodly do it', or something like that. I'd always sing it to my family. Although I was actually frightened of a lot of singing, the singing in school was jolly, whereas the music I was frightened of, like chorales, was somehow sad and creepy.

I moved up to Class 2. I quite liked it, even though it was in a different room with a different teacher. This is surprising, because any change in routine could really affect me. It wasn't too bad though, and at least in this class they didn't try to stop me from stimming. I still bellowed sometimes and kicked. For some reason I'd hate it when the teacher called me a 'good boy'; that would just make me shout. I can't really explain why I found it annoying – I guess I somehow found it patronizing and cheesy. Anyway, when I did get angry and yell, the teacher would claim she would send me back to Class 1 if I didn't stop, but she never did send me back to Class 1!

Before the school day was done, we'd often watch a film, 'You Can Read' – a sort of programme with lots of songs. It had one about a truck, and lots of others that I can't really remember. There was one I really hated called 'There's a hole in my bucket, Dear Liza'. I just hated it; in fact I was terrified of it! For some reason I found it so scary. I would wail for someone to take me out because I couldn't bear it. The teacher and all the teaching assistants would try to calm me down. I think they eventually succeeded, but as with the Halloween display, I'd only need to be scared of something once and forevermore it would haunt me. So, when the film was put on, I would always think that song would be played again and I would shout, "No Dear Liza! No Dear Liza!" and they would say, "It's alright Alex. We won't show you 'Dear Liza'". I don't think they did either – I think it was always fast-forwarded, but when I got home I still had nightmares about all the songs in the 'You Can Read' film – and I mean ALL of them, not just the 'There's a hole in my bucket' song! I can barely remember what the dreams were like, but I think I just about remember the first song about the truck. It showed clowns on the coach, with the noise of the coach getting louder and louder – it horrified me! I remember one dream I had was about a jester who walked into a castle, looked at me, and then opened a treasure box (or something like that). I know that doesn't sound particularly frightening, but I was petrified of jesters. Looking back, I don't think this was because of the 'You Can Read' film, but a CD-ROM that Ben used to go on all the time about castles and knights called 'Castle Explorer'. This CD-ROM had jesters in it and scary music.

By this time my language had come on a fair bit, although I stammered a great deal and still couldn't communicate very well. I could, at least, give a little insight as to what was happening with regard to my nightmares. One night, I got up and went into my parent's bedroom and woke my mum up. I explained (not as clearly as I'm telling the story now) that I saw all these pictures in my head when I was in bed, not knowing then that they were called dreams. She said, "Oh dear, I think you've had a disturbed night". I guess it was from then that she knew why I used to scream – but anyway, my mum put me back to bed and turned the light on because she now knew I was frightened. After that, I think the phrase 'disturbed night' became the thing that I'd say whenever I had a bad dream. I'd say, "I had a disturbed night!" to my mum.

CHAPTER 3
School at Home – Therapy Begins

Before I went to school, my mum had already begun to do some therapy work with me, but about 2 years later my parents decided to home-educate me; we began 'Applied Behavioural Analysis' therapy – ABA for short. ABA is specifically designed for autistic people. It aims to break down skills into smaller segments to be learnt and then put back together into sequence. It teaches things most people learn naturally by observation, but because the autistic world can be distorted and confusing, skills have to be learnt, rather than copied. My older brother and sister were home-educated, and my parents thought I should be able to join them as well. They had always felt guilty about sending me to school, yet my mum felt she would struggle to meet my needs without help.[2]

When I found out I was leaving school to learn at home I was quite glad. My mum told me I was to have two people working with me, Nicole in the morning and Kathy in the afternoon. I didn't much like them at first and when they took me out to teach road safety skills I wasn't co-operative, refusing to hold their hand, insisting instead on holding my mum's (who at that time always came with us). But in time they taught me to hold theirs and not to be so difficult – helping me to calm down and not have tantrums.

I didn't like most of the work, although they arranged fun activities too; they played pirates and 'action man' with me. My language was improving, although I still stammered repeating words like, 'but, but, but, but' at which point the therapists (and my mum) would say,

"Stop, think and then say it". I hated them doing that because I liked not speaking properly. Maybe I enjoyed being seen as a baby, even sometimes insisting I *was* a baby, speaking to my mum while she nursed Esther, pretending to be someone else with names like 'Baba' and 'Baby'. I really thought she thought I *was* a different person from 'Alex'.

There was something not quite clear to me though. I wondered how come I had people coming to work with me when my older brother and sister didn't. I was irritated that my behaviour was being controlled. At this point I had developed a broader range of films that I enjoyed, other than Thomas, and I would want to watch my chosen favourites over and over again, rather than work with my therapists. I don't remember much of those early beginnings of therapy, but my parents kept a lot of records of what happened during that time. I've read some of it, and that information has formed the basis for this chapter. The number of therapists increased – Heather, Sue and Zoe joined the team (I was excited about Zoe coming because one of my favourite characters in 'Sesame Street' was called Zoe, and I was totally obsessed with that programme then) – and they worked on a variety of activities like shopping, swimming, basic academics and social/life skills. I appeared to be making progress, although there were many problems still to overcome.

One area of difficulty I had was deciding what to do without being prompted all the time. They taught me to think through for myself what needed doing, and in what order, without being directed. For example, I needed to learn to go to the toilet without being told because I wouldn't go until I was prompted, by which time it was often too late. In fact when I went to bed I'd go to the toilet against the wall by my bed. I did it once and it seemed to work really well, so I did it again the night after and again and again. Eventually my mum found out and told me off – I didn't ever do it again, ever. It must have really stunk!

Socially I needed help too. One day Heather said, "Alex, we're going to take you to Beavers next week". I wasn't really sure what 'Beavers' was and I was really nervous. I remember the first time I went – Heather came with me because I needed a lot of help. When I first arrived and saw all the other children, I just wanted to get out – actually I don't think there were that many, but at the time it felt like there were a lot. The other children played games, but I didn't have a clue what to do, so Heather had to help me. Although I don't actually remember, my impression looking back is that I wasn't as scared as I had previously been in new situations. I certainly didn't scream to get out and, in fact, I think I quite enjoyed it. I would come home and then it would be explained to me how I did and how I could improve next time I went. I would practice all week how to have a conversation. I didn't enjoy talking to people and would prefer to stand and 'stim'. My therapists tried to get me to see that wasn't good and that I had to make the effort to talk and look interested (even if I wasn't!) because that was polite. I still find this difficult now to be perfectly honest.

Therapists came and went, and in due course two new therapists joined the team (Donna and Catrin), whilst Heather, Nicole and Sue left. Donna took over taking me to Beavers. She would often invite children back on 'play-dates' with me. I made friends with some of these children and got on quite well with them. If I made mistakes Donna would go over them with me, along with the other therapists, working on those areas I found difficult. For instance, they would let me know if my 'play-date' friend was looking bored with my conversation, or if I behaved inappropriately. I found it all a bit much; I wanted it all to end and to be left alone. Now I am glad they did work on these things because, even though I still struggle with social situations, it would be a huge problem if I hadn't gone through this.

The therapists taught me basic academics, like how to read, but I had trouble remembering which way round letters went, writing and reading a 'p' instead of a 'q', or 'b' for a 'd'. We had cards with letters printed on them, some written correctly (we called these 'good guys') and some incorrectly (we called these 'bad guys'). I'd have to look at them and say, "good guy!" or "bad guy!" within a certain amount of time. We also studied nature – which I absolutely loved. Catrin brought some tadpoles, which we put in a tank, and I would study them. I found that work really interesting – I thoroughly enjoyed learning about tadpoles and watching them develop. Kathy also did a bit of nature-work with me, and other sciences, reading books to me about how the universe works, plants and so on. However, on one occasion she mentioned there were slugs in our cellar, and that turned me right off of going down there because I was so frightened – which was a bit awkward because that's the main entrance out to our garden!

Difficulties arose when there were conflicts between what I *wanted* to do and what my therapists told me I *had* to do. I remember a time when I wanted to play 'shops'. We'd just bought this new game with a toy till, pretend money and everything, but Kathy said I should begin with spelling work. She then seemed to change her mind, and said we could play shops after all. When she told me we were going to play shops I started to scream, shouting, "I want to do spelling!" I actually didn't want to do my spellings. It sounds so illogical but I just wanted them to agree to do what I wanted. By the time they did say I could do what I wanted, I felt it was too late and wanted to make them agree to me doing something else. Well Kathy (and my mum!) was insistent that we played 'shops' and do the spellings later. My mum showed me the schedule, which was basically a timetable for work that I was going to do, and on it she had written down 'play shops' as a first activity and then spellings as a second activity. Beside the word 'spellings' she had also drawn a smiley face. Well that was it, I was incensed! I hated seeing a smiley face on the schedule next to 'spellings', because, in truth, I didn't want to do spelling, and the smiley face made it seem as though spelling was joy for me. I sound like a really spoilt brat, but I just hated being organized. I was being awkward, and now all these years later I can hardly remember why I reacted so badly.

Sometimes, I still feel like that now – especially when I've been misunderstood. Something happened much later on, when I was about 13 or 14 that shows what I mean. We went as a family to the supermarket, parking the car outside. I got out of the car, intending to walk around the car parking space to join the others. My dad thought I was just going to walk into the busy road and called out, "Alex, STOP! There are too many cars here!" He went on, "You see Alex, you were about to run into the road where there are cars". I said, "I wasn't, really. I was going to walk around the other side", meaning walk around the car parking space. I said it calmly, but inside I was boiling mad. I felt that my dad was treating me as if I were unable to cope with even crossing a road. I began to say 'autistic' stuff. It was a load of stupid things that I didn't mean. It's what I did (and still do now at times) to cover up my anger, but no-one guessed why I was talking like that. Some years after, I was telling this story to Annette, one of my later therapists. She explained that sometimes parents caution their children instinctively if they see dangers, without thinking their children may have already foreseen the dangers themselves. She said I had taken it too personally, and I think she's right. I thought he was saying that because I was autistic, but Annette said she thought he was reacting in that moment as any parent would. She said she did it all the time to her children, and that made me realize that parents say things sometimes to all their children, not just me. (However, I still do even to this day have a tendency to think people are patronizing me because I'm autistic, when actually they're not.)

About once a week (I think) the therapists would hold a team meeting. All the therapists and my mum, and sometimes my dad, would gather in our living room and discuss my program, thinking about what they needed to work on with me. In the early years a consultant from America would come and discuss my progress, and suggest the best way forward. I had definitely made progress – my speech and behaviour had really improved – but, as ever, there was still a lot of work needed. As well as the American consultant, the therapists had a therapy manager who provided regular support and advice as to what therapy was needed and would work best. She was an expert at helping children with autism and knowing what therapies were appropriate to help in different problem areas. Most of the time I stayed out of the way, watching a film upstairs or something similar. As a result of one of these meetings, it was agreed they were to begin teaching me what was nice to say and what wasn't. I had very little understanding of etiquette, being sensitive to another person's feelings, what was rude and discourteous or what wasn't.

I was shown two boxes, one had cards with 'nice' things to say; the other box contained cards with 'not nice' things to say. I had made some quite personal comments that were embarrassing and rude, even though that hadn't been my intention. This was intended to help me to navigate my way through conversations appropriately and sensitively. In the 'nice' box there would be suggestions like, 'What's your name?'; 'How old are you?'; 'What's your favourite film?'; 'What type of music do you like to listen to?' In the 'not nice' box there would be comments like, 'You've got a big forehead'; 'You smell'; 'You're fat'; and other things like that. I got an opportunity to put it into practice one day when Donna took me to the park with her daughter Faye and a boy from Cubs who lived quite close to Donna. While we were on the swings I was asking all the questions from the 'nice' box – which I guess was a good sign because it showed I was taking it all in.

My therapists would also practice the art of conversation with me. Two therapists would speak to one another and teach me to join in with both appropriate questions and comments. They'd get me to pretend to have a conversation with one of the therapists and see if I could ask questions and make comments. I tended to ask loads of questions, but not make so many comments. They would go over it with me again and again. I didn't really want them to, but I'm so glad now that they did.

I felt like I wanted it all to go away. I wanted to be normal. Looking back I think I gave everyone a hard time but I couldn't see that. I was just struggling to cope with all the demands that were being made of me. I still struggle to keep a conversation going and will really lose interest if the topic is something that doesn't grab my attention. My mum still tells me I must try to show an interest in what people are saying, but I find it really hard. My mind just wanders or I try to talk about something in which I'm interested. If I get onto a subject I'm really keen on I won't want to stop which apparently can be boring for people. It is just part of my brain being wired differently. I find 'normal' conversations boring and 'normal' people find my conversations boring. I also find it hard to think of something to say in time. Often by the time I have thought of something to say the conversation has moved on.

As a person with autism I always have to pretend to be something I'm not in order to be accepted. To carry on with a conversation I have to go into acting mode. This is always a big effort for me. I am often exhausted and will try to find a place where I can be alone to rest my brain and have a 'stim'. Most people take conversations for granted, but I find that whenever I've had a successful conversation with someone I feel as if I've done something amazing. I feel the same way that a normal person may feel when they've just passed their driving test. For me conversations really are that challenging!

I still went to church with my family. At this point, I didn't believe God was real because I couldn't see Him. I didn't even believe there were other countries or that the world was round. I remember learning that we all do wrong things, even our minister. This shocked me! Somehow I thought he must be perfect; he was God's spokesman and, in my mind, was much higher than everyone else. I liked the name 'Jesus', and some simple Christian songs would make me want to cry in a happy way. Some hymns even now make me want to cry, they are normally the ones my dad doesn't like. I found the sermons boring, yet I liked the way we always did the same things on a Sunday and the service followed a set pattern. I liked to join in with my older brother and sister as they talked to their friends after the service. I still feel accepted by those young people with whom I grew up in my church. Recently I spoke to my church about autism and belief. This was the hardest talk I have ever had to give. I knew they would have an emotional reaction. I found this difficult to cope with and embarrassing. Yet I felt it helped them to understand autism.

CHAPTER 4

The Doors Open

I wondered why my therapists were teaching me all these things. I knew they worked with other children, but those children couldn't talk, which didn't make sense to me. How come I was getting therapy when my older brother and sister weren't? How come all the other children taught by my therapists couldn't talk, but I could? Also, when I went to Cubs (I was no longer in Beavers) I was the only one who had someone with me – all the other kids were on their own. I noticed that I seemed to find things much harder than the other children did. All the other children just seemed to understand the rules of the games when I struggled to work them out. I started to think something was going on, but then I thought: "No! I have Donna with me just because she works with me, so she might as well go in with me…and I just find the games difficult because they are difficult…I'm probably just rubbish at games…everyone's rubbish at certain things! It's just that I'm like that".

I now had another baby sister called Alice. I insisted on her being called Alice. I just liked the name. But this has been a big mistake because since then whenever someone calls either of us we both answer. I found her really cute when she was born and I think I started to ignore Esther and I gave all my attention to Alice. I used to play daft games with Esther and Alice, like the game dinner. Esther would put spices on me and would be getting ready to eat me and I would try to escape without her and Alice noticing. I feel that Alice and Esther don't think about my autism so much because I was there first.

By this time Donna and Catrin were the only therapists working with me, Kathy and Zoe having left. I was sad when I found out Kathy and Zoe were finishing working with me – in a strange sort of way I had become fond of them. It wasn't long after this that Catrin left too. So, Donna was the only therapist left.

My mum began to look for new therapists to work with me. She asked a lady named Annette from our Church to join us. She was already a very dear family friend, and she readily agreed. I knew her as Aunty Annette, not because she was my Aunty but because we referred to adult members of the church as Uncle or Aunty. In fact, I still referred to her as Aunty Annette, even when she began working as a therapist – and do so up this present day (and in this book!).

Well, she began working with me twice a week. She took me to visit local historical places like Flint Castle and Basingwerk Abbey. Sitting together we would talk about what might have happened there in days gone past. I remember sitting in the ruins of Basingwerk Abbey where she taught me about Monks and the story of Martin Luther. Walking around Flint Castle she taught me about Edward 1st and how he built castles. I remember a book that told us about all the food they used to eat in the Middle Ages. It said they would cook a chicken in the oven and spice it. They would then use stale bread for plates and eat honey with the chicken. We decided to have our own Medieval Banquet at which Aunty Annette, Mum, Ben, Naomi, Esther, Alice and I dressed up in medieval clothes and ate medieval food exactly as the book had described. We had honey, roast chicken and even stale bread for plates. After that, it became a sort of tradition to have banquets that followed a theme. We had a Pirate Banquet and then an Egyptian Banquet – we were going to have an Indian Banquet, but somehow never got round to that. We kept that tradition for many years, having Banquets almost always before the summer break and Christmas break. They became something of a light-hearted celebration of forthcoming holidays, and something to which we all looked forward.

The therapists continued to have team meetings, overseen by Stacey, the new supervisor of the therapy program. I had improved enormously, but it was a work in progress and these meetings gathered everybody together to discuss current problem areas and ways to address them. On one occasion I was called into the living room to join them. I saw my mum, Aunty Annette, Donna, Stacy and another lady that I'd never seen before. Stacy introduced me to this new lady, "This is my friend, Roxie; we thought she could be a new therapist for you. Would you like Roxie to work with you?" She nodded her head whilst speaking to me, as if gesturing for me to say 'yes'. I hesitated – I wasn't really sure I wanted a new therapist, but it was obvious that she had come to work with me so I said, "Yes". "Good", said Stacy.

When Roxie started coming to work with me we found out she (like me) hated pop music. At this point music had become a bit of an obsession. I was obsessed with all different types of music and I kept asking questions about music to my brother, who was a bit of an expert. He was good at playing music, so I'd ask him if I heard music playing on the radio, "Is that classical music?" If he said, "Yes", then I'd usually like it, but if there was some modern classical music, sometimes I wouldn't like it and get very upset if, nevertheless, I was told, "Yes, that's classical". I think I liked to stick to rules.

Roxie did craft activities with me, and also took me swimming. After swimming she'd always buy me a Crunchie chocolate bar. She did therapy work with me and taught me manners. One day she was trying to speak to me and I was just humming a tune. She tried again, but I still kept humming. Finally she said, "Are you humming?" I answered, "Yes", to which she replied, "It's quite rude to hum when people are trying to speak to you!" I wasn't meaning to be rude; I just thought it would be funny to hum when people were speaking to you. I thought that was normal.

I had also taken up football lessons once a week. I noticed most children had someone there watching him or her from the balcony, but I actually had someone in the hall with me while we were playing football. The strange thing was that, although I didn't like playing the game of football, I actually liked going to football lessons. I wasn't any good at it (I'm still rubbish at it) and I guess that was why I had to have someone with me. All the same it didn't really make sense to me that I had to have someone with me and I hated it. At the same time I was aware that I found things harder than other people.

Occasionally, when I went to Cubs, Donna was unable to go with me, so Ben would go with me instead. That really made me anxious! What was going on? There was worse to come! My younger sister, Esther, started going to Rainbows (the girl's version of Beavers). She went independently, without anyone going with her. I asked, "How come Esther's going on her own to Rainbows, but I always have to have someone with me when I go to Cubs?" Naomi was in the car and she answered, "Because Donna works with you, so she might as well go with you, whereas no-one works with Esther". I wanted to say that, even when Donna wasn't there, they'd make sure someone was always with me, but I don't remember I got the chance to say that. It just didn't make any sense to me. There was a bit of me that liked Ben coming with me, because I liked him seeing what sort of thing I did at Cubs. However, I did notice that if ever I had been left on my own for a while, and Ben came a bit later, he would always ask the leader, "How's Alex doing?" and I'd overhear the answer, "He seems to be doing alright at the moment". I was starting to get suspicious, although I didn't suspect it was a disability, because I didn't really understand what disabilities were at that point, but I thought I wasn't right.

About this time I started to really get into the Chronicles of Narnia, and I began to collect all the BBC films (which is ironic because Narnia used to be one of the films I'd scream at saying I didn't want to watch it). In 'The Lion, the Witch and the Wardrobe', one of the children (Edmund) was nasty, and betrayed his brother and sisters by joining sides with the White Witch. It was one of the old laws of Narnia that a traitor must be put to death on the stone table, so Edmund had to be put to death. However, Edmund became truly sorry for betraying his family and was full of sorrow that he had ever been allied to the White Witch. He confessed this to Aslan, the Lion, who – although he had done nothing wrong – took Edmund's punishment and died in his place on the stone table. Aslan rose again from the dead the next day and lived forevermore in Narnia. This helped me to understand more about God. I had been told about the Lord Jesus dying for the wrong things I had done, but up until now it had meant nothing to me. From this time on I began to understand what that meant. This changed my thinking and I found myself able to believe in God. I also began to believe the world was round and that there were people in other countries. I was later baptized which helped me to be sure God loves me.

CHAPTER 5
Cool or Not Cool

My therapy continued, with team meetings being held periodically to discuss progress and ongoing problems. At one of these meetings, I was called into the living room where my mum, Stacy and all the therapists were sat holding little hands made of paper. Some of the hands had thumbs pointing up and some of them had thumbs pointing down. When I came into the room Stacy said, "Hello Alex, today we're going to be talking about 'cool' and 'not cool'!" They started talking to me about what things were considered 'cool' and what were 'not cool'. For example, 'not cool' would be humming when someone was trying to speak to you; interrupting when someone was speaking; asking questions, which were inappropriate; stimming when people were trying to talk to you. They told me that I should always think, 'is the thing I'm about to do, 'cool' or 'not cool'? Suddenly, they started talking about battles or something. Maybe I just brought the subject up randomly, or maybe I just don't remember now how it cropped up, but I do remember saying, "Battles are ugly when girls fight!" Stacy (the supervising therapist) was really offended by this – she thought it was a very sexist thing to say. Actually, I was repeating words from 'The Chronicles of Narnia' (the bit in 'The Lion, the Witch and the Wardrobe' where Father Christmas says those words to Susan and Lucy). I really didn't mean to be rude or offensive – I often did repeat things from books or films, in fact I think it was partly speech from films that helped my language to develop.

Whenever I said or did anything 'un-cool' my therapists would say, "Do you think that's 'cool' or 'not cool'?" and that was their way of trying to correct those socially unacceptable things I did of which, up until then, I had been unaware. On another occasion, when out walking with Donna and my sister Naomi, we started talking about fairgrounds and rides. Suddenly, I was out of the conversation and humming music by Bach. Donna said, "Do you think that's 'cool' or 'not cool'?" I said, "I don't know!" to which Donna replied, "That is really not cool! Why don't you join in with our conversation about rides? After all, you were joining in a minute ago". I had no idea what was so 'un-cool' about that – as far as I was concerned I was just showing Donna that I liked that classical piece of music, and I thought she'd think it was cool of me to hum it!

Looking back I think they were trying to turn me into something I wasn't. My mum says that she decided the 'cool' 'not cool' programme wasn't that good so it was dropped. It was around this time that I finished having ABA.[3] The consultant wanted to stop me from 'stimming' all the time and my mum felt this wasn't right. She was unhappy about only focusing on the external behaviours and not thinking about how I felt. I have anxiety about making mistakes and looking stupid. I wonder if this approach made things worse. I think you shouldn't try to change people from who they are; you should teach people skills to help them fit in. For a long time I was terrified of people finding out I had autism. I was worried they would treat me in a different way. In reality they probably knew there was something wrong after spending some time with me.

My family and I were members of an organization called 'Daffodils'. It was only for families who had a child or young adult with some sort of disability, and membership enabled us to go to places like Alton Towers, the Manchester Science Museum and other places, because the travel expenses and admission fees were subsidised. It was really good because they provided a coach right to the destination, and there were volunteers to help my mum because she had five children including me. One of the staff was a man called David, who we started to get to know quite well. He was very funny and jolly – always making jokes. My mum asked him to go with me to our church Holiday Bible Club, which is held every year during the summer break. The members of the church organize games and other activities for the children between age 5 and 12. David and I got on very well, so my mum asked him to work with me more often, doing therapy and other activities with me.

I really liked him; he was always 'pulling my leg' (not literally). Sometimes I thought he was being serious, but he helped me to understand humour; maybe that was the reason why my parents thought he would be able to help me. I remember when he first came that Esther was a bit frightened of him, and behaved as if he was a complete stranger coming to visit.

He took me shopping, and sometimes joined Donna as a sort of assistant. One day, when David was with me and my dad was there, he started teasing me, as usual. Dad said, "He's pulling your leg, isn't he?" David said, "No, I'm not! If I was pulling your leg, I'd be doing this" and with that he started to literally pull my leg. I thought that was really funny – he was hilarious!

By this time, I was getting too old for Cubs, but, as it happened, David worked with the Scouts at Sychdyn. It was because of that connection, that I started to go to Scouts there. There was actually a group of Scouts at Holywell, where I lived, but the meeting clashed with the night the young people from my church met, so David provided the ideal solution. Before I went Donna, Aunty Annette and Roxie started teaching me how to talk to people a bit better. I hated them doing this; I just wanted to be left alone and be the way I was. Donna came with me to Scouts, as she had done to Cubs. I was really bad at talking to the other children. Some of the children asked questions like, "What was it that made you come to Scouts?" and stuff like that. I answered their questions but looked away as I did so, not at all interested and showing it. When I got back in the car, Donna said that I hadn't done a very good job at socialising. I didn't like this at all; I didn't want to talk to a load of children I'd never met before and who were mostly older than me! When we got home I had a word with my mum about it and she said she'd talk to Donna because I really couldn't cope with it. For the time being, Donna stopped trying to make me talk.

It wasn't just the talking I found difficult. I struggled with the games, and it seemed so much harder for me to learn them than it was for most of the others. It sounds as if I didn't like Scouts very much, but actually I did. There was another boy I noticed who seemed to struggle too. If anything, he seemed to have more problems than me. There was one good thing though – a few of the children had their Mums with them – not for support, but to help out. Even if Donna was there to support me, she blended in better and it wasn't so obvious. I had improved since I'd been in Cubs and Beavers, and didn't need quite as much support as I had previously done with the games and activities. I was still learning though, one problem was that I couldn't listen to the instructions and understand what you had to do– even my name being called was hard to take in. Even now, I still struggle to grasp the rules of certain games, even when they're being explained to me. Overall though, I really did enjoy Scouts – the activities were varied and there were more of them than at Cubs and Beavers.

Meanwhile, David had got a new evening job at Daffodils, so he stopped going to Scouts, but there were three other leaders – John, Mike and Neil. Neil was a brilliant leader, and my favourite out of the three, but he wasn't there regularly because he had a job in Scotland. He got us working in groups and taught us geology. The first time I saw him I was a little bit scared of him because he was new (or new to me) and had lots of black hair, a beard, and he was a big guy. Almost at once though, I thought he was a good leader – he even taught me how to tie my shoelaces! He went over it again and again and, with Donna practicing with me at home, I eventually picked it up. Mike often expected a lot more than I was capable of me. I think I remember Donna saying that Neil had experience of working with people with disabilities, so that's what made him more understanding than Mike. John was also a good leader for the most part. Unlike Mike, he gave me a lot of support, but maybe a little too much support. There were times that I felt he helped me more than was needed, which made me stick out from the other scouts like a sore thumb - I think he was the 'main' leader out of the three. There were two other helpers who were from the Explorers Scout Group (the next level up from Scouts) and they helped to organize the games and other activities. Anyway, I believe the other Scouts guessed almost immediately there was something wrong, because they kept telling me what to do and giving me extra help. To be honest I needed it, but I didn't like having it. I just wanted to be like everyone else, and find everything easy.

David had by now left us as a therapist – he hadn't been with us long, maybe a few weeks, and then he finished.

CHAPTER 6
Changes Ahead

Instead of approaching any task randomly, my therapists began to encourage me to see that things had to be in order. For example, if I was going out, I'd need to get my stuff together: I'd need my coat, shoes and anything else I needed ready, so that I was organised. I had tremendous difficulty with doing anything in the right sequence. This was a problem, because otherwise I would turn up to Scouts or swimming without the appropriate gear. Roxie had borrowed some books from the library about cartoons, which showed us how to make our own flicker books and how to make Wallace and Gromit heads with modelling clay. The idea was that (although I wasn't aware of it at the time) it enabled me to see that for things to be completed successfully, there had to be 'order' – i.e. if the pictures were placed in the flicker book randomly, they wouldn't work. My dad got me a cartoon book of 'The Hobbit', where all the characters had speech bubbles. Aunty Annette came up with the idea of letting me write my own cartoon story – she says this was to reinforce the idea of sequencing and order. I made up the story and drew the pictures while Aunty Annette filled in the speech bubbles, which I dictated to her. I still remember how I used extracts from a mixture of familiar stories: the pebble trail from 'Hansel and Gretel'; the toffee tree from 'The Magician's Nephew'; Bilbo, Gandalf, Frodo and the rings from 'The Lord of the Rings'; gifts from 'The Lion, the Witch and the Wardrobe'; some of Gandalf's speech were quotes from 'The Silver Chair', and so on. We really had fun doing that cartoon work; it did help me to see the importance of being organised, and it was to lead on to a deeper interest in animation.[4]

Stacey, the supervising therapist had left at about this time and a lady called Carole replaced her. She used a therapy called Verbal Behaviour. I was much happier with the new approach; they used natural environment training to engage my interest. I thought I was having fun, while all the time they were teaching me things. At, I think, the first team meeting to which she came, I was called in and she put on a video of 'Pingu'. That made me very happy. Even though 'Pingu' wasn't exactly my favourite film, it was definitely therapy I could enjoy! She kept stopping it and asking me questions about how I thought the characters were feeling at certain points in the story. My mum now says that it was to help me understand how other people feel, and maybe they thought it might have more of an impact if they did it through a video – and, I have to say, I think it helped.

Aunty Annette brought some tadpoles in plastic bottles from her pond for me to see. We put them in a tank in the garden. Soon after we dug out a pond in the back garden, ready to put the tadpoles in. Aunty Annette says this project was designed to help me with planning and sequencing. We had to figure out where best to dig the pond, what size and shape the pond should be, which pond liner we would use and how much we would need and finally, how much it would all cost. We went to a local garden centre and did a bit of research. As it so happened, my parents had a builder in to do some work at the front of the house, and he gave us some plastic liner that we were able to use which was a big help. At the team meeting following the completion of our pond, Carole and the other therapists came out into the garden to see it. Aunty Annette and I had made a plan: We knew Donna hated holding frogs because she thought they were slimy (secretly, I have to admit, I agreed!), so when we all got to the pond we planned on giving Donna a frog and Carole some tadpoles to hold. Aunty Annette said we should say to Donna, "We know you love nature *so* much, we would like you to hold one of our dearly beloved frogs." However, I went and spoilt the plan because I just went up to Donna and said, "I want you to hold one of my frogs, and if you do, you shall be given a reward". Donna looked very nervous, but when Aunty Annette caught a frog and gave it to her, she managed to hold it. When we put the frog back I said, "Now…. your reward is…for Carole to hold a tadpole!" Donna wasn't terribly impressed, but I think overall my evil plan worked! Joking aside, I wasn't aware of this at the time, but I've heard that Carole was really encouraged that my language skills were improving. I absolutely loved our pond and I enjoyed talking about it and telling others what we had done. There was always something new to say about it as well because it was evolving and changing throughout the seasons of the year, which kept the conversations new and fresh.

Meanwhile, Roxie had finished working with me. As a farewell present, she got me a Crunchie chocolate bar, because she knew I liked them.

I remember learning about people from other cultures. We used to read a book called 'Window on the world' and I was fascinated by it. I found it really exciting to learn about other ways of living. I would flap my hands when people were dressed differently; I liked learning about all their different religions. This led to a special interest in places in the world. Particularly where they were and what continent they were in. I also became really good at knowing where countries were on a globe. I had a CD with geography songs on it. I loved to listen to these songs. I also had a talking globe: it had a special pen and could tell you the capital of each country. It could also tell you the Prime Minister or President and (my favourite part) a piece of music from each country. I loved listening to music from all the different countries, particularly music from the Middle East. I was interested in everything from the Middle East. I thought the Middle East had a very interesting culture; I loved the rich clothes they wore and, as I mentioned before, the music to which they listened. One of the countries I always wanted to visit was Egypt. I wanted to see the pyramids and the famous Tomb of Tutankhamen. I remember finding out about Rameses II, I saw a picture of his sarcophagus. I was so excited to think that he may have been the Pharaoh who wouldn't let the children of Israel go. I thought this because I had watched a few videos of the Moses story ('The Prince of Egypt' to name one), and in these videos he was called Rameses.

I loved learning different parts of history particularly the Kings and Queens of England. I liked learning the different ages of Britain such as the Celts, the Romans, the Angle Saxons, the Vikings, the Normans, the Plantagenet's, the houses of York and Lancaster, the Tudor's, the Stuarts, the Hanoverians and the Victorians. I can still roughly name all the Kings and Queens of England in order, or at least from William I onwards. I liked the Tudor's and the Middle Ages because they had such exciting stories. I liked to visit the art gallery because I could see paintings of these historical characters (although I found the statues embarrassing, and if you've seen many statues, I probably don't have to tell you why). For a long time I liked to show off my knowledge when I was there.

If I found myself in a lesson of no interest, I couldn't concentrate at all, and I still can't. Even when the lessons are of interest, my mind wanders. I learned by doing; if something interested me I would keep on repeating it in my head because I was so excited about it, and I would keep on stimming over it. I might even pretend I was in the history about which I was learning. I didn't sit any formal exams because I couldn't follow the questions and recall the answers. I found the questions used language that I couldn't process. I find it hard to answer questions and bring up the right piece of information, even if I have the knowledge. As I write this I even find it hard to recall what I have done today, and I always used to find that when people asked me "What have you done today?" I always used to respond with "All kinds of things". People would reply, "Like what?" I couldn't recall exactly what I had done, so I'd say "All kinds of things" again. When I was 15, I decided that saying "All kinds of things" never seemed to be of any use so I stopped. I no longer say that. However, I might say, "Not much", which seems to get me out of it more often than not. I find it easier to recall things when they just come out naturally.

On one occasion it was coming up to Donna's birthday, and her television had broken, so I wanted to replace it as a present for her. I spoke to her about it, and although she said it was an extremely touching thought, and very kind, she told me that it would be far too expensive and couldn't be done. I didn't understand money: For me, expensive things were just things that I wanted, but wasn't allowed. I'd often see something I liked in a shop, ask my mum if we could buy it, and she'd say, "No! It's too expensive." I didn't really understand why, or what that meant. Anyway, I suggested to my mum that we buy Donna a new TV for her birthday, and she gave me the same answer Donna had done, that it would be too expensive. I think it was at that point that my therapists and my mum decided they had to teach me how to handle money. Actually, I'm still learning how to manage money because I'm really bad at maths. It is one of my weakest areas, and one with which I'm still struggling. I started to learn money skills, and, even though it's still difficult, I would never make that kind of 'television' mistake again. I now understand that there are some things which really are too expensive to buy.

CHAPTER 7
My Differences Become Apparent

I definitely made a lot of progress in the five years from when I was, I think, 6 to 11. I was taking in most of the therapy and understanding it. I still didn't like some of the things they got me to do, like when we went out shopping to practice money skills. The therapists and I would go to the shops, and they would tell me to buy certain foods, without telling me exactly where in the shop I should look for them. They would give hints as to the general direction, but I would have to locate and pay for them myself, which I found really annoying. I see now it was probably for the best because I did need to learn how to buy things for myself. Coming home in the car I was very quiet because I felt very annoyed with my therapists. I think Aunty Annette knew, because she remembers that we bought mint ice cream with which we made our own McFlurry to cheer me up (McDonald's McFlurrys were a favourite of ours). I think it worked, because I certainly remember making it, I just don't remember it was at that time or for that reason. We made them at other times too though, quite a lot!

I described at the beginning of this book how terrifying I found everything about a trip to the shops: the music, the dummies, the lights and the people. They all scared me. Well, by this time, although I still found it all very daunting, I coped an awful lot better. I no longer screamed, even though I still found the music horrible, especially if it was a large sport shop and the music was extra loud. I definitely no longer thought there were gods in there. I didn't think the lights were pop stars on the roof singing – now I would actually pray to God that the shop music wouldn't creep me out.

I went to this club, which I called 'Thinking Club'. It wasn't actually a real club; it was where I would sit down, usually in my room, when the day was finished, or during the day if I had time, and think about things in my past and stim over them. I developed an excellent long-term memory, rehearsing in my mind past events, keeping memories in my head because it made me feel really happy. I would also pretend things happened, which hadn't. Every night I would collect all my thoughts that I had kept in my brain and put them on a list of things to think about. I decided other people went to 'Thinking Club' as well – mainly quiet people. I would repeat conversations that I had heard, or that I had had, whispering words over and over again, at the same time stimming. I had always done these things, but it was only recently I began to think of it as a sort of 'club'.

I don't believe it is right to stop me stimming all the time. I think it needs to be controlled in public places, but not stopped because it does provide a focus for me. Stimming in the wrong place or at the wrong time, could worry or embarrass other people, or possibly make me vulnerable to bullying so I try to control it when I'm out. If something exciting happens, I'll stim discreetly by holding my hands low down and squeezing them together, or grabbing on to my knee. Alternatively, if I can go somewhere private, I'll have a good stim on my own where no one can see. There are lots of different types of stims, and they're not all the type I do when I'm thinking about the past. When I'm bored I stim in a different way - I fidget all over the place and put my head down, not managing to hide it very well. In fact, everyone has some sort of stim. Sometimes it's foot-tapping, finger-nail biting, twiddling with hair or fiddling with things. People do these things when they get nervous or stressed. Aunty Annette fiddles with her hankie: She twists it and sometimes she isn't even aware she's doing it.

I'm like that when I chew paper, or start peeling bits of wood. It's done subconsciously. That's not part of my 'thinking club' stim, it's just something I do without thinking and hardly notice I do it.

I also had a few health problems that impacted on my behaviour. I am allergic to wheat and if I ever ate anything with wheat in, it would make me feel sick, and I would act in a more autistic way. I had severe asthma, and if that worsened, that also would affect my behaviour. What made it worse was that when my asthma was bad, I couldn't really communicate with my parents and tell them what was wrong. The most I would say was, "I'm not feeling well." I wouldn't be specific. One day I had an asthma attack, coughing all the time but just telling my parents I didn't feel well, without saying in what way. My asthma had been bad for a while, but I hadn't said. If I'd told them, it could have been sorted, but I'd left it too late. I've since been told I have 'silent asthma' where I have an awful lot of trouble breathing, and I wheeze, but only I can hear it. However, no-one else can, so they are not alerted unless I explain what's happening.

On this particular day I was feeling really bad. My parents kept asking, "Are you feeling wheezy? Are you finding it difficult to breathe?" I just said, "Can't you hear me?", but they said they couldn't, which I didn't understand; after all, if I could hear it, why couldn't they? Eventually, they decided to take me to the Cottage Hospital where the nurses listened to my chest and realized I was finding it extremely difficult to breath. They put me on a machine to help me to breathe. I hated that machine and, as far as I remember, it didn't work anyway as by then I was too ill to respond. The hospital finally decided they should call an ambulance to transfer me to a big general hospital. My mum came with me.

When we arrived I think I was put in a private room and given an oxygen mask as well as other things. A nurse came in and asked to take some details, which my mum supplied. She mentioned I was on a gluten free diet, but she also spelt out some letters, which the nurse wrote down. The letters were A, U, T, I, S, M. When I heard that, I wondered what it meant, but assumed it was something to do with the gluten free diet or something and just ignored it. A while later, another nurse came to take some details and again my mum mentioned I was gluten free and spelt out the letters. This happened one more time before I was put on a ward. I think it was then that the doctor came to see me, and he asked for details. My mum replied, "He's gluten free, and he also has A, U, T, I, S, M". This time I noticed the doctor looked a little curious, almost as if he wondered why my mum didn't just say the actual word. My mum said, "I can't say it because...." She didn't really say any more than that, but the doctor wrote it down, but said out loud one word: "Autism". Afterwards I decided I wanted to hear more. Once the doctor had gone I asked my mum, "What's this A, U, T, I, S, M you keep talking about?" She said, a little awkwardly, "Well, um, err, it spells 'autism'. It sort of means that you have certain things you find difficult... You have some difficulties". I think I related it to the other children with whom I knew Donna and the other therapists worked, and I said, "But, I can talk fine". My mum explained that it wasn't just about the way someone talks. She said that although some autistic people couldn't talk, some *could* talk, but just found certain things really hard.

I didn't know quite how to react to this. On the one hand, it explained a lot, like finding things harder than other children or having to have someone with me whenever I went anywhere. It also explained why I actually had therapy in the first place. On the other hand, surely I didn't have anything wrong with me; I couldn't be autistic! I decided to ask my mum more questions, still insisting I couldn't be autistic, because I could talk fine and everything. She said, "Alex, it isn't about the way you talk. There are people who talk really well who have it. All the people in your old school have it". I mentioned a few that I thought didn't, but she told me they did. She told me a boy that went to our old church, a friend of Ben's, had it. He talked really well, and I would never have suspected he was autistic. When I heard this, I thought, 'no, he doesn't have autism', but I said, "Oh, he can talk alright". My mum said, "Yes, Alex, he can talk really, really well. If you want I can try and get him to come over and talk to you about autism, and he can tell you what his difficulties are." I agreed to him coming over.[5]

My mum said, "I was going to tell you when you were older about the cause of your difficulties, so you could understand it better. That's why we give you therapy, and why you find it difficult to make friends. People with autism find it difficult to make friends. Donna says there's another boy in Scouts who has autism." Straightaway I knew to whom she was referring. Somehow, we got on to the subject of 'Daffodils' and I asked her if that organization was for people with autism. "Well", she said, "it's for people, with all kinds of special needs." "Oh, right", I said, "So there are other 'special needs' as well? What are their names?" My mum mentioned a few people we knew who had disabilities and what the disabilities were called.

When we returned from hospital and I was feeling much better, my mum made the arrangement with Ben's friend who had autism to come over so that we could talk about the difficulties we each had. Some were different, and some were the same. When he came, I was thinking, 'he's not autistic, he can't be', and when he left I told my mum that he didn't have autism. She told me he definitely did. After I heard he had autism, it made me feel a bit more comforted.

In fact, in some ways I felt better because I knew what caused my difficulties. After seeing this boy, I felt like I was the same as everyone else, except I just had certain difficulties. However, one bit of me still didn't believe it was true, because I could talk fine and didn't look disabled. Was it really a disability, or was it just who I was? On the other hand it explained a lot. For a long time now, I had had a sense that something wasn't right. Why did I have therapy but my siblings didn't? Why did I always have to have someone with me? Why did I find things harder than everyone else? At the age of 11 I finally had the answer. It explained why I went to 'Thinking Club', though from that time I no longer thought of it as a club – I thought of it as an 'autistic box' where I stored pictures which I would go and open at times in the day when I was on my own or mostly at the end of the day. It would be like opening the box and taking out all the pictures, looking at them, stimming over them and replaying them in my mind.[6] I still didn't really understand it. One part of me didn't want to have it. Another part of me felt it was good to have something that made me different from other people. Sometimes I doubted I had it, other times I knew I had it. I understand why my mum wanted to wait until I was older to tell me. I now know for definite I have it. I definitely have a disability which is autism, but back then a bit of me still didn't believe I had it.[7]

CHAPTER 8
My Life Takes a Turn for Clay

Throughout this account I have tried to retell my story as it happened – or at least as I remember it happening. I've tried to work out exactly when events occurred. Sometimes I have guessed a little and used logic at times when my memory is a bit fuzzy. The next couple of chapters cover roughly the same time chronologically, but follow different aspects of that period of my life.

My family got a new laptop, and I was very interested in it. Carole (the consultant) suggested I should have one of my own, and it was agreed the program would pay for it. Some time later we went to see a new 'Wallace & Gromit' film called 'The Curse of the Were-Rabbit'. I remembered that when I was younger that Ben and my dad loved Wallace and Gromit, but I had never been a massive fan. In fact I couldn't even really remember what it was about, except Wallace went around in massive trousers! I knew Roxie liked it too, and after I went to see this latest film I could see why. In fact, I enjoyed 'The Curse of the Were Rabbit' so much I wanted to see all of the Wallace and Gromit films. I bought them for my dad for Christmas and became pretty obsessed with them and the actual animation technique used to film them, stop motion animation. This technique involved plasticine models being photographed repeatedly, they were then moved slightly each time a photograph was taken. Once all the photos were put together and played at speed, the effect was given of the character really moving, and that's how they made 'Wallace & Gromit' – although some of the later ones (I think) used a little bit of computer generated imagery for certain parts of the films. I decided I wanted to make my own animation about Scudder, the imaginary character I decided was responsible for many of the bad dreams I'd suffered (along with 'the wolf' and 'Scrap Trevor') when I was younger. I used to play games about Scudder with my brother and sisters. We'd pretending Scudder had died and we'd go to his funeral. It would then it would turn out he hadn't died after all. It was a good game and Scudder was to be the subject of my first animation. I wanted to have a wolf in the story trying to sleep next to this little boy to frighten him, but there were three problems: I didn't have any plasticine, I didn't have any wire for the plasticine, and I didn't have the software with which to film it. However, I had already thought of a way round that! I thought we could buy plasticine and wire and, instead of the software, we would use the 'flicker book' principle. With help from my therapist, I'd buy the plasticine, make the models and, using a normal camera to take photographs, I'd make a flicker book. I would then record the flicker book using a video camera. If it turned out the way I imagined, it would look like a proper animation. A few days later, Donna said she saw some plasticine in a shop in Holywell, so we bought it along with some wire. It was only a cheap packet, with a small strip of each colour. I managed to make half a small dog for the 'wolf' character out of two colours, but there really wasn't enough, so my dad looked on the internet and found a website that sold massive packs (I think it was manufactured by the same company that provided the plasticine for 'Wallace & Gromit'). My dad ordered me some plasticine. He also told me he'd noticed on the website that you could buy your own software as well. "Oh.... can we get some?" I asked - I was really excited. My dad said we could, but not right then. I now went off the original plan of using a flicker book and video camera. I desperately wanted this software!

Soon, the plasticine arrived. It was fantastic and included a massive pack of each colour. I made another two models and completed the dog. I don't remember why, but I changed my mind about making Scudder the subject of the film. I decided instead to make it about a man called William and his dog, Dylan. I constructed another character, but it somehow got ruined, so a friend of mine repaired it, by which time it looked nothing like the original – more like a small monster. I decided to call him Patrick, the Big, Bad, Creepy Monster. This was even though he was quite small and Patrick, the Small, Bad, Creepy Monster might have been more suitable even if a bit cheesy! I began to plan the film! I wrote the script – it was about people in a railway station being attacked by Patrick, and a man called William saving the day with Patrick ending up in prison. I drew some pictures of what I wanted the people in the railway station to look like, and Aunty Annette and two friends helped make the actual models, as well as two black dogs and a human head on a spidery body (which we later decided would make a better Patrick because it was bigger and looked kind of scary). (See Appendix 1)

Soon after this my mum started looking at software prices on the Internet and found the cheapest was, I think, about £100 for the junior version. We talked about it and my mum said that because it was so expensive I'd have to wait until my birthday, which was a long way off. I protested that I wanted it then, but she said I'd have to wait. I was worried that she would forget by the time my birthday came, but she promised me she wouldn't. I didn't understand that some things cost too much to have straightaway. There was quite a lot of arguing, but I did agree to wait, although I took a lot of convincing! Whether I liked it or not, my parents said I had to wait until my 13th birthday, so I had no choice but to wait and hope they wouldn't forget!

I began to write the script and plan the film in earnest. I was still pretty bad at sequencing. I had to do a storyboard for my animation, and I think this process helped me to understand the need for sequences. I wondered what to do with the first model of Patrick and my dad suggested that it could become Patrick as he ends up: defeated and small. I decided Patrick would go to a land called 'The Land of the Dead Wasp', this was after seeing a dead wasp get caught in a bottle of juice as we travelled along in the car! I divided the script into scenes, I won't tell you the whole story here, but I loved making the film. If you're interested in reading a brief summary of each scene, check out the appendices at the end of this book.

I enjoyed writing the script, making the models and planning how we were going to film it all.[8] In the meantime my birthday was getting closer and closer. One problem I kept thinking about though was how we were going to film a railway station. We needed a building but I wasn't sure how we were going to achieve this. One day, Donna and I were walking in town when we came across an architecture practice, and in the window was a model house. We wondered if it would be worth asking if they could make us a model railway station. Donna made enquiries a week or so later, and the architects that worked there were very helpful, so we both returned and spoke to one particular man who agreed to build us a railway station. Apparently, he made model buildings for his own amusement but so far had never completed them. We weren't sure how much it was going to cost. The man who said he'd do it wasn't sure himself. The owner of the practice said it could cost a fortune, which made me very nervous, but finally it was agreed the man would do it for £80 which was still a lot of money, but far cheaper than we had first thought. We went home, discussed it, and eventually it was agreed that I could get one. The man started work on the model and emailed us to keep us up to date with progress. He suggested we pop in from time to time to bring in some of the models we had made to photograph alongside the railway station. It was looking very good.

I added one of the stages to my blog I'd created not long before. I think it took some weeks to complete, but when we went to see the finished model it was brilliant! He had made it the perfect size and, better still, it would be useful for future animation projects in addition to this one. It could be almost any building – a church, hospital, or even a mansion-style house – it was absolutely fantastic! We were all really pleased with the man's work – it couldn't have been better!

CHAPTER 9

Life Skills and Wonka Bars

By this time I had been having therapy for about 6 years and had made lots of progress. My language had improved a great deal, and I could now speak pretty much fluently. Nonetheless there was a big difference between my language in a social setting and my language at home. I still didn't like speaking to people much and still tended to look away during a conversation, but I was getting better. For instance, when I went to Scouts and got to know a few children a little bit, I began to grow more comfortable talking with them. I still wasn't very good at it, but I was better than before. My therapists were still working on problem areas with me as I was slow to develop some skills that my peers had already nailed. For example, I could tell the time, but had little sense of time. I was very slow at routine practical tasks, often daydreaming and taking more time than necessary to get dressed, take my inhalers, get washed, etc. I wasted time stimming and would think about things a lot, which would distract me from everyday tasks that were important and had to be done. My therapists began teaching me to have a better sense of time and to stay focused on whatever I had to do. Money skills were still a big issue because I still didn't really understand that either, so that was another area on which my therapists concentrated. I remember when the Tim Burton version of 'Charlie & the Chocolate Factory' was coming out in the cinema and all the shops were selling Wonka bars. Donna and I were in Woolworths and she said I could have one if I wanted, but she would use some maths skills with me in order to do so. I think the Wonka bars cost 50p, so when Donna got some money out and asked me quizzically, "Is this enough?" I assumed it was, and said, "Yes". Donna gave me the money and sent me to pay for it. I went to the till, showed the lady the Wonka bar, and gave her the money Donna had given me. The lady looked at the money and said, "This isn't the right amount". I said, "Yes, it is". Donna said, "Are you sure it's the right amount?" I said, "Yes!" The lady insisted it wasn't the right amount and I insisted it was. Finally, Donna said, "Look at the coin, Alex! Is that enough?" I looked at the coin and hesitated, "Yeeeaaaah, Nnnnnoooooo....Nno....No." I realized it wasn't a 50p, but a 10p. I was so disappointed. I guess Donna was rather embarrassed by this and apologized to the lady. We left the shop without the Wonka bar. The truth was that when Donna originally showed me the money I didn't really look, and that was the point that she was making. I just didn't notice she had given me a 10p rather than a 50p and that was the challenge she'd set me, to see if I would be able to recognize the difference. Because the coins are both the same colour, and roughly the same size, I just assumed I was being given the right coin and only realized it wasn't when it was pointed out to me.

Another area of difficulty for me was forward thinking. I would often run out of inhalers, because I didn't tell anybody I was running out until it was too late. By the time a prescription request was submitted, picked up and dispensed at the chemist a few days would go by when I would be without medication and my asthma would worsen. My therapists started teaching me to recognize when I was running out and to communicate that to others. I didn't like people seeing me use my inhalers (I still don't now), so it was important for me to say when I needed a new prescription.

I also struggled with reading, writing and spelling. My mum says she asked an educational psychologist to assess me for dyslexia when I was younger. He had concluded that I just had generalised learning difficulties. However, in order to help me with my word and letter recognition we used a book called 'Toe-by-Toe'. I really hated it. Even so, I have to say I probably did benefit from it, because it involved reading columns and columns of sounds and words over and over again. I especially hated it when I had to read this dull book aloud to lots of people and it really embarrassed me. However, no matter how much I hated that book there was at least one way it helped me an awful, lot that was in letter recognition. I still often got letters mixed up, but this book taught me how to remember the right letters – like where there were two pictures, each of a ball and a bat. One showed the bat before the ball and the other the ball before the bat. It was a way of remembering the difference between a 'b' and a 'd'. It said bat before ball was 'b' and ball before bat was 'd'. I also got mixed up with 'p' and 'q' (although not quite so badly because I could at least remember that 'q' has a little line and 'p' doesn't) – although that didn't stop me from writing the letters the wrong way round. 'A' and 'E' were another two with which I'd struggle. Carole, our consultant, recommended a book designed to improve language and thinking skills. It was called 'Language for Thinking'. I absolutely loathed that book! It seemed to me to either teach very basic things I already knew, like the days of the week or the months of the year, or things I didn't need to know, like synonyms (two words for the same thing). I found it extremely dull, although, in fairness, I think this book also helped me more than I was actually aware. My younger sisters, Esther and Alice, joined in these lessons and we nicknamed it 'Language for Boring'! It came with a workbook and instructed absurd things like colouring the tree blue and stuff like that. I guess it was designed to help with listening skills, so that we followed instructions rather than assuming we knew what would be asked of us. I hated almost all of it – all except one called 'absurdity'. You were shown a picture of something extremely silly, say, a horse in a garage, or a car inside a house. You had to look at the picture and say what was absurd about it. I knew a horse in a garage was extremely silly, but the thought of it was quite funny, so I quite enjoyed the 'absurdity' chapters. Around the same time, I began to help my youngest sister Alice with her work, listening to her read amongst other things, because my mum thought it would develop my explaining skills and in turn help me learn as well.

Donna was also encouraging me to be more independent. I was going into the shops and the Post Office by myself. I didn't really want a lot of independence, but of course, I didn't know I needed to learn these things in order to be more independent when I got older. I thought it'd probably just happen, just like it did with other people – I didn't think I'd have to learn it. She taught me more Road Safety. I was slowly learning – my mum was so pleased when she found out I'd been into the Post Office by myself while Donna waited outside.

CHAPTER 10

Juggling Sandwiches: The Tale of an Awkward Teen

Socially, I was also improving. I still found going to Scouts extremely hard, but I was better socially, verbally and practically. When I first went to Scouts I really didn't want to talk to anyone, but by this time I did and was at least making an effort. This was even though I still found it very hard to fit in. I looked at all the other children and knew how different they were from me. They were often silly and messed about, whereas I was always very well behaved and rarely got told off. This was one of the many reasons why I couldn't fit in. When they told jokes I didn't know how to react – I can't deny this is something I still struggle with today. Anyway, I looked at everyone else messing about and doing silly things and decided it might help me fit in better if I tried being more like them. I still literally didn't have the ability to properly socialize, but I tried whenever I could to be like them. I have to admit now that this was a bad idea and didn't work. The fact was, I still wasn't doing it right. I just did it about different things, and at the wrong time – like Mulan in the Disney film. She was a girl in the army pretending to be a man, trying to act like she was the same as any other men. If you've seen it, you'll know she didn't get it right; she just came across as odd. Well, it was like that with me in Scouts; I tried to be like them, but it was even worse than just being me and not speaking to anyone. I came across as weird. Sometimes, as I talked, they looked at me suspiciously, like they knew there was something different about me. I didn't dare tell them about my condition because I was frightened they would treat me differently. I remember one time we were out on a hike. At lunchtime I was holding my sandwiches when one of the Scouts said something like, "Alex, have you got your sandwiches?" I said, "Yes! Maybe I should try juggling with them". He just looked at me and said I was weird. I must admit that would have come across as weird, but I was just trying to join in the banter and the messing about – but I just couldn't get it right. The older Scouts knew I had a problem (I think) because they had been there when I was much worse. The newer Scouts also knew there was something odd about me, but I didn't want to tell them the truth. I was too frightened. Even though I was having all these problems, I enjoyed Scouts and was a lot better at understanding some of the games – although I was still terrible at football In fact, I'm still pretty bad at football now! I was glad I was interacting a bit better – even though I was still really shy when everyone was talking to each other and found it very difficult to join in. In fact, I still do, even now. The fact was I would either appear incredibly quiet or just really weird – I often couldn't tell if the Scouts were being sarcastic either, especially if they kept a straight face.

There were a few occasions in Scouts when I was very embarrassed at being so rubbish at things. There was a time when they were all doing map reading. There were two groups: one for the older, more experienced, Scouts, and one group for the younger ones, who had just moved up from Cubs. I was one of the older ones, but because I didn't understand map reading and was slower to pick it up than most of the others, I was put with the younger ones. I was so embarrassed – I would rather have been put with the older ones, even if I didn't have a clue what was going on. Anyway, the leader started explaining the map reading to my group (the younger ones) and he said, "When you get to sort of 12/13 you'll be able to use these on your own". Well, when I heard those words, I felt even worse. I was 13 at this point, and still hadn't been able to learn it. One of the younger boys started speaking to me and he asked how long I'd been going to Scouts. I was quite embarrassed, but I replied honestly, "Ages! I've just never picked up map-reading!" He asked me how old I was and I told him I was 13. He looked at me as if that was pretty bad that I hadn't learnt it by my age. He said, "13?" almost looking embarrassed for me. "Yes!" I said – I was just ever so embarrassed! I suppose I should have told him the truth about my condition, but I just wanted them to think I was normal – just like them. Perhaps it would have been better if I had told them – they probably would've found out I had problems later anyway, and they already knew there was something very odd about me, so why not? If I didn't tell them, they'd likely think I was just flat-out thick, so is it really any worse for them to know that there's a reason for the way I was? To be perfectly honest, I still don't like people knowing sometimes.

To help with my independence skills, Donna encouraged me to take responsibility for paying my own subs to the Scouts. Every week she would give me the money from to pass on to the leader. Every week I paid. I'd have much preferred for Donna to do it, but I now know it was for the best. One week we were doing some cooking outside and the cheque for my subs was in my pocket. We cooked all kinds of food, like sausages-on-sticks and marshmallows. I was really enjoying it. I noticed some Scouts emptied their pockets of paper things like tissues on to the fire, so I copied them and did the same. One of them started asking me loads of questions; he clearly knew there was something different about me. I told him I was home-schooled and that Donna was my teacher. He asked how many floors I had in my house, but I misunderstood the question and mentally started to count up carpets (because you often refer to the carpet as the floor). So, in my mind he asked how many rooms there were in my house, not how many floors. I said, "7" and he looked really amazed. "7 floors?" he said. "Yes" I said. He replied, "Wow, that's amazing". He went and told one of the others and he also was amazed – I guess they thought I was rich, living in a house with 7 floors! When the day was over, and we were about to go home, Donna said "Well, Alex, you'd better give your subs to the leader". "Ok, I will" I said, but when I put my hand in my pocket to give him the cheque, my pocket was empty! I couldn't believe it; I panicked. I told Donna and the leader that it was gone, so we decided to look for it in the woods, where we did the cooking. The leader got a torch and started searching. Fortunately, it was only a cheque, so it could have been worse, but we still needed to find it. We looked everywhere, but it was nowhere to be seen…and then I remembered something, "Oh", I said, "I've just remembered! I emptied my pockets of paper and put it in the fire!" Donna replied, "Alex! You haven't!" "I'm afraid I have! I didn't mean to. I forgot about the money, I was just trying to burn my tissues!" Donna replied, "Well, Alex, that's it then, we'll have to go home". She turned to the leader and apologized, saying "I'm just trying to give Alex the opportunity to do things for himself." I can't remember what we did about it, whether Donna paid him then, or we paid extra next week – but I do remember feeling very bad about it. Anyhow, we got into the car and Donna drove away – but there was worse to come! As soon as we got back from Scouts, I remembered the question one of them had asked me and it suddenly dawned on me that he hadn't meant 'how many carpets do you have' but 'on how many floors was my house built?' I had completely misunderstood the question. I think it took me a while to process what he meant, but all I can say to that is, "No wonder they were so amazed!"

Meanwhile, I had finally got the software for the animations – and it was quite good.

We decided to attempt some simple, short animations to begin with and then perhaps to tackle my 'Patrick' film as we built up our expertise. We found, however, that even really short animations (I mean only a few seconds duration) took a very long time to compile, and I realized it must have been really, really hard work for them to make 'Wallace & Gromit', especially 'The Curse of the Were-Rabbit', and that it would be extremely difficult for us to make my 'Patrick the Big, Bad, Creepy Monster' animation. We kept encountering so many problems, like, for example, recording a soundtrack. Aunty Annette (who worked with me) often took my laptop home with her to see if her son (who's an expert on computers) could help us sort out these technical difficulties. We had so many hiccups trying to sort out the sound, amongst other things, that weren't available on the junior version that I was using. We didn't know how to export videos to computer files, so we could only watch them using 'Stop Motion Pro'. This meant we couldn't upload any of them to YouTube or anything. Overall, we enjoyed it, but it was hard work, challenging and sometimes very frustrating! I didn't know there was actually a much easier way of doing it either – we could have just used a normal digital camera, putting all the pictures together into a film with 'Windows Movie Maker'. I hadn't even attempted animations using plasticine yet – it was really too hard to work with – even though it would be a blockbuster if I ever managed to do it with 'Patrick, the Big, Bad, Creepy Monster', wouldn't it? I still hoped I could continue to build up experience and knowledge enough using one plasticine character with 'stop motion animation' and could then going on to do more. I didn't know when that would be, but I hoped 'Patrick' would become a reality one day!

CHAPTER 11

I Am Not Alone (Or Gonzo and I Understand Each Other)

Every Tuesday I went horse riding. It was held at stables specifically used by people with disabilities and it was a rule that you had to telephone to say whether you were going or not. Donna thought I should start phoning them up myself, so every week Donna would arrive and give me the phone to use. I hated it – I didn't think I was old enough to be phoning up people. I told Donna I shouldn't have to be phoning people until I was 18! Donna said I should be fully able to do so at 14, which if I'm not mistaken wasn't far off. I now see it was for my own good, but I didn't back then; I really wanted Donna to continue to do it for me. The fact was I didn't want to be independent yet because I thought it would come automatically, although there were some things I did enjoy doing on my own. For example, I attended a drama group at Mold Theatre every week for people with disabilities and I liked it when my dad dropped me outside and let me walk in on my own. That made me feel independent, so I guess in some ways I did like a drop of independence!

We were still working hard on the animations, but were having lots of problems with the computer. It kept crashing without warning and then the sound went, so we couldn't really use the laptop any more. I think we might have got Aunty Annette's son to look at it – I don't remember – but even if he told us what was wrong, he couldn't fix it himself so we decided to get a new computer. I really wanted to get the new Windows Vista to see what it would be like – it looked really cool! We emailed 'Stop Motion Pro' and asked if the version I had would run on 'Windows Vista' successfully. We were told not, but there was an updated version that would. I also wasn't sure if the webcam I was using for the animations would work on Vista, because it did actually say, 'Windows XP´ on it. We went to a computer superstore and asked one of the assistants for advice and, as far as I remember, he didn't think 'Stop Motion Pro' would run on Vista either. I think when we left the shop I mentioned that an updated version of 'Stop Motion Pro' would run on Vista, and so my parents phoned Aunty Annette who confirmed what I'd said. I can't remember how soon it was, but I did get a new computer. We installed 'Stop Motion Pro' and also decided to continue using my old webcam to see if it would work, which it did, very successfully! We found the webcam was not only good for animations, but for recording films. We started to do some recording of us all and I said lots of funny stuff. My mum started to record each of us individually as we talked about our own thing. I talked about animation – I've accidentally deleted what Esther did, but I know Alice talked about stories. At some point, Donna called to take me to Scouts and I showed her these recordings before we left the house. Some bits showed me laughing my head off, and Donna liked them, but what we didn't realize was that it had still been recording when Donna arrived. When I played them back again the following day, it had recorded me shouting "Donna's here!" and me telling Alice to open the door!

Now we realized the potential of the webcam, we started filming loads of funny plays and sketches. We made a very funny tramp sketch as well as newscasts and all sorts of other things. I sometimes did videos just recording myself and saying all sorts of funny things and pretending to be evil villains who were going to take over the world. It was great!

The animations were better on the new computer because it was much more powerful (in fact, I had this computer for quite a few years and when I first started writing this book, was still using it, although I now have an Apple Mac).

We still had difficulties to overcome, but at least the computer didn't crash every 5 minutes!

Still working towards independency, Carole decided I should apply for a free Bus Pass. Although I had to have someone with me, Donna agreed that I should have one so that she could accompany me and help me practice using public transport, with a view to my using it when I was older on my own.

I also used to study current affairs as part of my school curriculum. During this lesson my mum would read all kinds of stories from the newspaper to my sisters and me. One day, she read about this autistic man by the name of 'Steven Wiltshire'.

He could do fantastic art work, drawing buildings absolutely precisely, reproducing every single detail with perfect accuracy. All he would need to do was look at the building for a few minutes in order to do it. He drew it so precisely that it looked like a photo had been 'photo shopped' to resemble a drawing. It was indeed perfect! After my mum finished reading, she asked, "Do you feel proud Alex, that someone who has autism could have such a brilliant ability?" I said, "I'm sure plenty of people have a gift like that who don't have autism!" She said, "No, Alex! Not who have a brilliant ability like that". I was quite impressed by this. My mum looked him up on YouTube and founds lots of interesting videos about him and his art. When we'd finished our school work that day, I went back on YouTube and looked up more videos about him. I was familiar with YouTube as I often watched videos about Lemony Snicket and 'A Series of Unfortunate Events' (which was an obsession of mine at this point). However, as I started to watch videos about Steven Wiltshire, I saw other related videos on autism and began to click on them. There were some about other gifted autistic people, for example, a man who could calculate very easily, and another called 'Autism & Me' which I found very interesting. From there I got on to videos about Asperger Syndrome (which is a high functioning form of autism). I remember one called, 'In My Mind' which was very good – I recommend you check it out (if it's still there by the time you read this book), because it is absolutely brilliant! The username is Alex Olinkiewiz if you're interested.

These videos helped me to feel less alone. It felt as though I had finally found other people like me. I felt almost like Gonzo in Muppets from Space when he finally found the other members of his race. Before I found them, I felt like Gonzo when he said 'Well, it's just that I'm sick and tired of being a one-of-a-kind freak, that's all.'

Well, by now I was 14, in my last year of Scouts and improving all the time. We were divided into groups, with each group having their own Scout leader, usually one of the older ones, who were responsible for putting up the flags and running the games. My group was called 'Wolves' and I became the leader, although I didn't run the games, because I couldn't really explain them or get them into line when it was time to fall in. I was still extremely shy, but people didn't think I was as weird as they used to when I was 13. I think now that not many of them noticed I had a disability. One thing, which made it better still, was that I didn't need as much support from Donna. She still came, just in case I needed to have something explained to me, but by now she had become a helper and so some of the Scouts didn't even realize she was there for me. A lot of them saw her as one of the leaders, which, from my point of view, was really good. I was even beginning to understand the map reading a little better!

I also started to learn how to ride a bike. I know it might sound quite bad that I was 14 and still couldn't ride a bike, but I used to have quite poor balance skills. I had started to do equestrian vaulting (gymnastics on a horse) which had helped my balance a lot, so we thought maybe now I could learn to ride a bike. Before this I had only ridden a bike with stabilisers – without them I'd get frightened of falling off.... and would fall off. Now I started to learn without stabilisers and believe it or not, I did do quite well. I picked it up fairly quickly (thanks to the vaulting) and rode around the place without falling – it was easy!

Returning to independency (this is going to sound so embarrassing), I was now also learning to run my own bath. I know it doesn't sound right at 14 to be unable to run your own bath, but that was what I read in a report about me from that year. I think the reason why I couldn't was because I just couldn't get the water to the right temperature. I would put the hot in, then the cold, but it'd be too cold, so I expected others to do it for me. One day my mum showed me how to do it and I decided to give it a try. I now see it as a piece of cake to run a bath, and feel kind of embarrassed when I think I didn't learn it until I was that old!

Sometime after this, my mum found out about a programme called 'The Learning Breakthrough Program'. It was designed for people who had one or more bits of their brain that weren't working as well as other parts. It was basically a load of exercises where I'd hold onto a ball that was attached to string (whilst balancing on a board) and hit the ball, keeping my eyes fixed on it. The idea was to help me to focus on things I found difficult, using the bits of the brain that aren't affected to help the bits that are. This was known as brain plasticity – the theory that the brain can rewire itself after it has been either damaged or has some bit of the brain that finds something difficult. Not so long ago, my father had a stroke and we tried it (as well as other therapies) on him and it was pretty successful. Anyway, when I heard about this, I got pretty excited! Soon after it arrived, I tried it out and after a week it did seem to have an effect and appear to be working. I actually started giving a bit of eye contact to people after doing this, whereas before I never gave eye contact. I didn't even realize you were supposed to! It also helped my writing – we looked at some of the earlier essays I had written. They were pretty messy and the spelling was simply awful. After these exercises I would say I was slightly better, and improvement continued. I'm still not exactly an expert at spelling, but at least most people can read what I write now. I wasn't even able to spell things like 'though' or 'knee', so this balance program certainly has helped quite a bit.

CHAPTER 12
My Best Friend is a Web-Cam

The more I watched the films I made, and thought how funny they were, the more I thought it would be a brilliant idea to upload them on to YouTube. I had by now seen lots of videos about autism on YouTube, and many people with high functioning autism or Asperger syndrome had posted videos explaining how it affected them. I decided I would do the same, so I signed up for YouTube with the username 'Sitheis' (the name of a character in one of my stories). I tried to upload a video, but I was unable to because my email address was protected by parental control settings. My mum suggested creating a new account, but that meant I would be unable to use 'Sitheis' as a username, and I really wanted my username to be Sitheis! I decided to leave it, although I was desperate to upload some videos. However, I did settle for making a playlist with other people's videos instead, for which I didn't need the email permission. I knew that most likely I'd just have to wait until I was 18 (which was still 3 years off), because then the parental control setting would be removed. When my mum saw the playlist that I had done, she thought the videos were mine, but they weren't. I made a couple of films and put them on my blog. When my mum saw them, she wondered why I hadn't uploaded them to YouTube, so I had to tell her I still hadn't solved the problem. One day I hit on the idea of creating a new account using my mum's email address. I chose the username 'Sitheis2009' (because it was 27th March 2009) and it worked! I uploaded lots of films I'd recorded and made new ones. I created videos about autism and posted responses to loads of videos about autism and Asperger's, including the video 'In My Mind'. I was enjoying this so much. In fact, I think uploading videos to YouTube became a bit of an obsession. I was always doing it every day; uploading loads of videos. Whenever I saw a comment on any of them, I got really excited because it proved people were actually watching them. I even got a few messages and friend invites from other people with autism. I seemed to be helping other autistic people to understand themselves. I think it also helped some parents of autistic children to understand their children better.

However, looking back, I do think I said a lot of things in those videos about which I have since changed my mind. For example, in one of the videos I said I was fairly independent. I now see that was not so. I was aware I was kind of slow to learn independence, but I thought I was more independent than most autistic people. I knew I struggled with money, but felt that other than that, I was ok. However, I may have had all the basic skills in place, but I didn't have half the skills I needed to live a normal life. This is hard for me to admit and accept even now, but we're still working hard on independence. I'm trying my best and that's what matters, and I can actually do a bit more now than I could then. Often, I'll be quite stressed that I can't do things that other people can. In another of my videos, I pretty much implied that autism was hardly a problem to me anymore. Yes, I still had it, but I had learned to live with it, making out that it mostly affected me socially. That isn't true either, even though I wish it were. I knew I did find things harder than other people, but I didn't imply that in my videos. But anyway, I'm not being big-headed or anything, I do think I helped a lot of people. Before the channel got closed, I had over 100 subscribers to my YouTube page. That shows my videos must have been popular.

Other people with autism were helping me as well. I knew I had autism, but I didn't really know much about it. I knew it meant I had difficulties with certain things, and I knew it meant I found it hard to make friends, but apart from that, I was pretty ignorant about the condition itself. These videos really helped me to know more and understand myself better. I heard some people say that autism should not be cured and is a gift. This helped me to see that autism wasn't necessarily a bad thing, even though it can be annoying and difficult! It has its good parts too. I found that joining YouTube also helped my spelling a lot. I'm still not an expert by any means, but I was getting better, and still am. I used to be so bad that when I wrote a story, I would have to have someone check it thoroughly and do a lot of correcting. However, by this point I think people could read what I wrote pretty easily and my punctuation had improved too. I could pretty much correct my own spelling, except if the spelling was so bad it wasn't in the spell-checker. I think it helped that I was getting a lot of comments on YouTube and I began to recognize words and learn how they were spelt as I read them. The balance board helped too. I also had a blog (well, I still have it) on which people commented. This all encouraged me to read and spell accurately.

I had actually had this blog since 2005, originally to post about electronics, but a year later I started to add information about the film I was planning to make. I stopped adding to it until November 2008, when I started up

One day, when I was looking at the videos my subscriptions had uploaded on YouTube, I spotted one of them was an animation about somebody with Asperger Syndrome. The voices sounded weird, like robots, and it said 'Xtranormal' on it. I noticed, in the related videos, others that looked and sounded similar – posted by other YouTubers – and so I decided to look up 'Xtranormal' to find out all about it. It was a free online animation program where you could choose actors, scenes, little things for the actors to do and ... (this is the coolest bit)... you simply had to type in what you wanted your character to say, and he/she would say it! You could even choose what accent you wanted your character to have – isn't that neat? Of course, it had its limitations as well: you couldn't make the characters walk, you weren't allowed more than two characters in one scene and the robotic voices sometimes didn't sound right, even though the idea was very cool. As soon as I saw it, I realized that with this software I could make my 'Patrick, the Big, Bad, Creepy Monster' film which I'd wanted to make for 2-3 years. I had to change the script a bit – there could only be two characters per scene and, because there were no 'monsters' as such to select, I couldn't have the bit when Patrick turns into the monster. I changed it so that he got a new costume instead that gave him powers. I also changed the title to 'Patrick the Traitor'. Most unfortunate of all was that, because the characters couldn't walk, I had to make them dance.

CHAPTER 13

Cameras and Holidays (Or How Two Seemingly Unrelated Things Are in the Same Chapter)

I haven't yet mentioned my interest in photography. I had got a new camera and would often go to places and take photos. One day my mum, my two younger sisters and I were sitting in a Café-type place, when we noticed some courses advertised. When we looked, we found a part-time photography course. It was held at that very venue where we were. My mum thought it might help me with my photography, so she decided to talk to Deeside College about it. It turned out to be stuff I pretty much already knew, for example, how to turn on the camera or import photos to the computer. Anyhow we decided it would be best to start at a basic level and build up my knowledge from there. I'm not quite sure how it happened but I assume my parents spoke to Deeside College, because we went there and told them I was interested in doing Level 1 Photography at the Holywell campus (the Café-type place). We explained my interest in photography, computers and what you can do with cameras and, of course, (not to my pleasure, but still the right thing to do) we told them I had autism. One of the men who worked there said, "From what you've told me, Level 1 is much too easy for Alex! Level 1 is literally how to turn the camera on; it's for complete beginners who don't know anything about photography. Alex should do Level 2". I think my parents asked of what Level 2 consisted. They were told, something like, it was just the next level up, and that it was held at Deeside College and not the Holywell campus. My parents decided to enrol me on this course instead. I asked them, "How difficult is it?" I think they thought I was worrying, but actually I think I just asked that because I felt I ought to contribute something to the conversation as I thought I'd been a bit too quiet. Anyway, the man said, "It's not that difficult; it's only the next Level". My dad enrolled on the course too, in case I needed a bit of extra help – but at least he enrolled, rather than just accompanying me, so it wasn't like, "Hey everybody! Look! I've got someone with me! I've got Special Needs!" Plenty of fathers and sons enrol on courses together, so nobody would think anything to it. Even if they did, they'd probably just assume I was underage (which for the first month I was, because I was still 15). I turned 16 in October, so even if I hadn't had 'special needs', I would have needed to have someone with me for that first month.

Because my dad and I had enrolled on the course, we decided we needed a better camera. I already had a camera, but it was only a cheap one – well, not cheap, but it was only a little one and not a professional camera. As we wanted to get a professional camera for the course, my dad said, "Alex, we need to look on the Internet for good cameras". I didn't really know much about what we needed, but I thought it sounded good, and I looked forward to getting one. We thought we should go for a second-hand one, otherwise it would be too expensive. However, in the event the program provided the money, which meant we could afford to get a good one that wasn't second-hand. After looking on the Internet, my parents found a Nikon D60 camera, which is a very good camera, so they ordered it.[9] A few weeks later, when it arrived, I must say it was very posh. I looked at it, but my dad had to show me how to use it because it had different settings for people, plants, landscapes, animals, sports as well as other subjects. It had a little eye to look into so that you could see the subject of the photo. It also came with a lens that you could use if you wanted to zoom in or out, which is a technical way of saying, 'make your subjects appear nearer, or further away'. I could go on, but I don't want to bore you, so I'll leave it there for now!

Social situations were still a problem, as they are now. I was a bit better at talking to people one-to-one if I'd known those people for a long time, and if they made an effort to include me. I was still pretty bad with some people. Sometimes I wanted to socialize, but that didn't mean I could. The same is true today: even though I think I have improved now, I still struggle a great deal socially.

In social situations, I would often just watch other people talking and want to join in but, somehow, I couldn't. To give you some idea of what I mean, let me tell you about a home-schooling holiday we went on at about this time. On the first day, I went into this room where the teenagers' Bible talk was progressing. I sat down, but I was so tired that I couldn't really follow it. Anyway, when it finished we went outside and all the teenagers were together, chatting, but I just kept out of the way. About an hour later, I was still doing nothing – just walking around the campsite, doing nothing, I kept walking around and around in a circuit. I had been to a different home-school holiday before. They had been a bit boring, but at least there were things to do on the campsite! This had nothing. I was bored stiff! You either socialised or you were bored – I was bored. Unfortunately I had forgotten to bring my brand new camera. Had I brought it with me, it might have helped and given me something with which to occupy myself. My mum actually came up to me and asked if I'd like to join in with the teenagers. The truth was that I did, but somehow I didn't feel like they'd really want me to join in. The whole time, I really hated it and this was only the first day! I was homesick already! Soon after, my mum asked if I'd like to have a rest and listen to my audio book. At first I said no, because it was a rule in my head that I had to listen to the audio books only in the night, but my mum said it would really help, and almost insisted that I did it. I gave it a try and it turned out to be a big help.

When I finished the audio book, and had a little rest, I went out and felt much better. I even did a bit of archery (at which I was terrible, but that's not the point) and spoke to some people. I think soon we went out to get something to eat and I spoke to my family then. The next day I still hated it (I think), as I looked at all the other teenagers talking to each other while I was just sitting out. What I didn't know until writing this book was that my parents had a word with some of the other parents about my problems. This led to some of the teenagers going out of their way to include me. I had decided to go into this building and the teenagers there started to speak to me and, over the next couple of days, there were more activities, so I had a better time and began to join in more. I was still quiet, but at least now I wasn't just walking around on my own for hours. By the time the holiday was over, I found that I had actually rather enjoyed it, and I went the following year as well.

About a month later, we went away again on holiday. This time I had remembered to bring my camera. When we arrived, we had a lot of trouble putting up the caravan awning because the wind was very strong. Eventually, we managed it, but it didn't stay up for long. Poles kept falling down and one night the whole awning collapsed again. With difficulty we got it back up but again it came down. It happened again and again! Eventually, we told the farmer about it and he brought a rope and a tyre to keep the awning up (it fell down again when we left, but that didn't matter for obvious reasons).

Anyway, after we'd arrived and put the awning up, I went around the campsite taking photos. My dad had shown me how to do it and, in no time, I was pretty much addicted. We started to go to lovely places so that I could take loads of photos. We went to the beach so I could photograph the sea, sky and everything. It was amazing, and I was beginning to take some good shots.

Stimming was a bit of a problem when we went away camping like this. I can't cope without stimming and, when I'm at home, it's pretty straightforward because I'll go into a room on my own, think about what I've done that day, while I do strange movements. But, in a caravan there's nowhere to go to be private – there just isn't the space. Well, I decided it'd be a good idea if I went outside, behind the caravan – so that's what I did. I stimmed and stimmed and stimmed; repeating all the exciting things I'd done that day, stimming about things I planned to do, pulling and fiddling with my piece of string, whispering, rocking and hand clapping. I really went for it! All of a sudden, this chap came up to me, looking pretty worried, and said, "Oh, are you alright?" I think he thought I was having some kind of seizure or something! "Yes", I said. "Are you sure?" he asked. "Yes!" I said. "I'm a friend", he said, "If you need any help, then let me know!" Later, I think he had a word with my parents about it and I think they explained I had autism – I suppose I really should have told him, but there you go. I reckon my parents were embarrassed about it because they said, "Alex, don't you know that lots of people can see you out there?" I explained I usually had a good stimming room at home and there was nowhere else I could go. You can see the funny side, but socially you can probably imagine the awkwardness!

Well, when we were going, we got everything packed into the car, hooked up the caravan. Typically we needed the farmer to tow us out, and off the campsite. It's a shame I didn't take a photograph of all three engines being pulled by each other, for it was quite an interesting sight and no mistake!

CHAPTER 14
The Tale of a Three-Headed Ghost

So, as you heard in the previous Chapter, I was enrolled and due to start the Level 2 Photography Course at Deeside College. Now that the start date was approaching, I was getting really nervous. I somehow thought when I was enrolling that by the time it started, I would be ready, but now that it came to it, I wasn't ready, although one bit of me was still very excited. Typically, I do get this mixture of emotions whenever I start something new – nervous and yet excited at the same time. However, I was especially nervous with this because I was possibly going to be the youngest there, it being an adult course.

On the first day, when my dad and I arrived, I saw everyone else and, as I had suspected, they were all a lot older than me, with the exception of one lad who was about two years' older than me. Well, the lecturer arrived, took the register and we began! He talked us through the basics, for example how to turn the camera on and how to import photographs onto a computer, saying this was Level 1. I was a bit confused because I thought it was Level 2 and would be harder than this, but he went on to say we would be covering some Level 2 stuff, so it would get more complicated. When we left, I remember thinking, "Wow! That was easy! I don't think I'll have anything to worry about on this course. It's going to be easy!"

The following week we covered a little bit on Photoshop and how to edit photographs. We went downstairs where someone volunteered to have their photograph taken and then we returned, imported the photos to the computer and edited them to improve any imperfections.

I was amazed by some of it! There were some blurred photos, yet with the Photoshop software you could improve the quality so much that, in the end, they looked really good. Obviously it had limitations and some pictures were so blurred you couldn't sharpen them up that much, although you could do other things with them. For example, one picture was so blurred (I think the camera had been shaken or something) it looked like a picture of three men, rather than one. I put eyes on each head of the man so it looked like a kind of three-headed ghost! It was really cool (even though I say so myself) and, when the others saw it, they laughed, including the man of whom the picture was taken and my dad. In the car on the way home, I was thinking about the course and how good it was.

The next week, it was much harder. Our lecturer was teaching us all about the capabilities of the Photoshop software. I can't remember the details, but I do remember he did a really cool thing on our computers. All of a sudden, we saw our mouse move and the computer was doing stuff, even though we weren't moving the mouse. Through this, he was showing us what we were going to be doing on our computers. However, I found this really difficult because I couldn't remember all those instructions. By the time the tutorial was finished, I had completely forgotten most of the information and didn't really know what I was supposed to be doing. Worse still (but better in a way!) my dad was lost as well.

Well, when we left that last class, we came out of the building, got into the car and drove away, still unsure of what to do about the second course, whether we should do it or not.

One day, I was just hanging around in the house when my mum said something along the lines of, "Alex, you know you can do Stop Motion Pro on your camera?" "Really?" I asked. "Yes," she said. I decided to check it out – I thought maybe I could swap the webcam for the camera when making Stop Motion Pro animations. However, when I looked I found you could actually do the whole animation just using the camera – technically it wasn't Stop Motion Pro, because that's a software program, but the camera had a facility very much like it. This was really cool! This would be easier to add sound to as well. It was really difficult getting sound on the Stop Motion Pro animations. I decided to have a go. I got the camera, but I was a bit unsure of how to put it into the stop motion format.

On, I think, the next day, Aunty Annette came, had a look at it and sorted it out. I could be wrong – my memory isn't too clear on this – but I definitely do remember making an animation almost at once. We used a doll ('Gabriella' from 'High School Musical') as a lady, a large chair as a cliff, and we had this monster push her off the cliff. It was a *really* bad animation – very shaky – but it was a 'first attempt' and I knew next time to use a tripod or place the camera on a flat surface to avoid that problem. I did other animations – such as a banana peeling itself – and I began to think once again that maybe now, just maybe, I would get to make my 'Patrick, the Big, Bad, Creepy Monster' film, after all!

Not long after, I started a course on horse care every Friday. Two years previously, when I was coming up to 14, I had started vaulting. I decided to do a course in horse care that the RDA (Riding for the Disabled Association) ran. It was a lot easier than the Photography Course, it being (as I understand it) specifically designed for people with disabilities. It was a far more practical course than the photographic course, and I found it a lot easier academically. In fact, I really enjoyed the academic side of the course, as well as the horsy bit.

The one thing I did hate was the lunch hour. I *love* eating good food, but I hated the lunch hour because after I had eaten my lunch, everyone would just sit down talking, and I got really bored by that. I just wanted to go out and do more work. Because I have autism, I'm not a massive fan of social chitchat. I much preferred to be getting on and doing more work with the horses or more of the academic work.

Before I started the course, I was extremely nervous, as I almost always am when starting something new (I have a bit of a fear of failing, and get easily embarrassed when I make mistakes, so when I start somewhere I'm always like, "Oh…. just supposing, I make a real fool of myself"). Actually, I get nervous, to a lesser extent, even when I'm on my way to somewhere I go every week, because, unfortunately, it is quite common for me to make mistakes! At least, I feel as if it is and I almost always relate my mistakes to my condition. People always tell me that anyone could make a mistake like I make and, while I believe that to a certain extent, I think I especially make mistakes. Some of the mistakes that I've made are so stupid that I find it very hard to believe that just anyone would make them. I also tend to worry that people will look at me and think I'm quite thick, but I'm learning that other people don't usually think like that, and I'm learning to overcome this anxiety.

Anyway, despite this, I quite enjoyed the course. I have now finished the course and have gained my NVQ level 1 in Horse Care.

CHAPTER 15

A Battle For the Ages (The Snowman vs. The Stupid Fork)

About two months later it was Christmas time and we were all opening our presents. When I opened mine, I saw that it was an animation model - it was bendy, so that I could move it, put modelling clay on it, or just animate it the way it was. I was pretty pleased with it.

Soon after, I started making an animation without modelling clay, just using the model. I decided to make the model into a kind of skeleton in the film. In the film a 'thing' starts to walk towards the skeleton, but the skeleton shoots, with a gun, and the 'thing' dies. I put it on YouTube, but unfortunately I no longer have that account, so it can't be seen there any more.

Soon after I made an animation using the model, but this time used modelling clay to cover it – I decided it would be about a snowman. I said to my mum one day when it was snowy, "You know, I fancy doing a snowman animation". My mum said, "That'd be pretty difficult, the snowman would probably fall apart!" "Not a real snowman!" I said, "A modelling clay one!" My mum said, "Oh, a modelling clay one, right." Almost at once, I began covering the model with the modelling clay. I used several sets of white, and hoped to have enough left over for a background of white snow. Unfortunately it was a tight stretch and there wasn't enough, so I had to be content with using tissue as the snow on the floor. I added plasticine eyes to the model and a hat and scarf. It looked pretty good. I started to make the animation, taking photos of the model and moving it a little each time. I made him a little fork out of clay, which would keep following him. Eventually, the snowman threw the fork out of the way, and then it jumped back and the film ended. I watched it when it was finished, and I thought it was pretty good – maybe a little fast-moving, but still good.

This time, I decided to add speech to it, but there was a problem because the snowman's mouth didn't move. Donna said that that made it more 'snowman like'. I thought that was quite illogical myself, but I went with it, because I really wanted the snowman to have speech. I started recording my voice for the animation, tapping my desk to make the sound of walking (even though it wasn't that reliable). When the fork came towards the snowman, I made him say something like, "What! I'm getting rid of you…. stupid fork!", and then, "Don't Come Back!!" The fork comes back and the snowman says, "WHAT?!!" and then it finishes with the credits. I did the speech a few times to get it perfect. When it was completed, I watched it, uploaded it onto YouTube and most, if not all, of my subscribers saw it, and liked it. My mum shared it on Facebook too - it really was quite good, and there was better to come!

When I next went to my drama group we sat (as we often did) in a circle and went around saying what we had done that week. When it was my turn to say what I had done I said, "I've made two animations at home". The lady who ran the drama group said, "Really??" I said, "Yes!" She said something like, "That's awesome Alex!" I told her that I'd put them on YouTube and she asked if we should go upstairs to the office and see them, right then and there. I said, "Yes, alright." So we went upstairs, put YouTube on and I told them the names of my animations – 'The Shooting Skeleton' and 'The Depressed Snowman'. We watched them and when they were finished everyone looked really impressed and complimented me on them. A few of the helpers gave me comments like, "Wow.... I could never do that...I literally wouldn't have the patience to do that". Those comments made me feel very pleased.

I was 16 by now, and had full knowledge of my condition – I didn't doubt it at all. When I was 11, I thought something wasn't right, but now I knew for definite that there was a problem and, even if I had never been told, I think I would have figured out for definite that I had some problems – although I'm sure my mum would've told me by then anyway. She did say, when I was told of my condition, that she had wanted to wait until I was a bit older to tell me the truth, but now I was aware that I'd need a significant amount of support to get on in life. The year before I had just kind of thought (or at least hoped) that I'd keep on making more and more progress until I had more or less caught up with everyone else, but I was beginning to see that that wasn't the case – I'd need an awful lot of help to be even a little independent. I had now started having my own money, but my parents were managing it – it was extremely hard for me to accept I couldn't manage it alone. I was still having therapy. Well, it wasn't so much therapy now; it was more just help with Life Skills.

By now Carol Roxburgh was no longer supervising the program. We had a team meeting with my mum, Dad, Aunty Annette, Donna and my sister Naomi was in the room as well. By now it was thought I was old enough to join in with the meeting, since I now wanted all the help I could get so I could get as much out of life as possible. Previously, I had wanted the therapy to go away because I didn't understand how much I needed it. Even though it was hard for me to accept now that I did need it, I knew the more help I refused at this point, the more I would need it later. Anyway, don't you think I should get on with what happened at the team meeting? Well, I'll tell you. We were all sitting, discussing what we should be working on next. We decided that catching buses would be a useful skill to have. This required even more work on my money management skills, for even at this point my money skills needed a significant amount of work. My sense of direction needed to be developed and worked on so that I would learn to look around when I went out to avoid getting lost. Social skills were also on the list, as well as hazard awareness (as I'm not really very aware of hazards, although I think I'm a bit better now than I was then).

We're still working on a lot of these things no – they made it very clear to me that I'd never be able to do things I wanted in life unless we worked very hard. Even then there were no guarantees, since some of the things were/are really big struggles (like maths). We'd been working on maths very hard, and I still only improved a tiny bit each time. Anyway, we all agreed to work on my money managing skills and Donna suggested that when I turned 17, I'd be better with money (although not much better with maths!) and that I would know roughly how much money was in my wallet. We'd also do 'shopping practice', and even though my maths is very poor, I think I have made progress. I think part of why I find maths so difficult is that I lose track of what I've just added or subtracted. However, I can remember people's ages, when I haven't seen them in years, and work out how old they would be now. I also often remember what years certain films came out in.

One day, they asked me "Alex, how much money do you have?" I said, "I don't know". My mum said something along the lines of, "But Alex, I told you to keep track by writing it all down". I replied, "You said nothing about writing things down; you just told me to keep track of how much and I find it very difficult to remember". My mum said, "Well, Alex, most people would take 'keep track' to mean writing down, so please do that". So, I started trying to write things down, although I didn't keep it up for very long, however, we continued working on my money skills!

Meanwhile, my interest in animation continued. I decided I wanted to do an animation about Count Olaf from 'A Series of Unfortunate Events' – I was really into this story at this point and wanted to make Count Olaf make a speech and, if possible, with his mouth moving because I really didn't think it would look right if not. Say what you will about the snowman, at least snowmen aren't really alive, while this was an animation of a human being. I'm not saying the character's real, but men are real, and it really wouldn't look right in an animation of a man talking if his mouth didn't move. I knew it would be difficult. I believe in the making of Wallace & Gromit they used separate pieces of the head and mouth on sticks so they could keep using different mouths, but I couldn't really do that, since my animation model already had a round head. So what could I do? Well, maybe I could have two lips on the head that keep moving; it'd be difficult but worth a try. However, when I looked in the animation box for the clay, I remembered I had used all the white up, and realised I could probably do with some flesh-coloured clay. There wasn't really enough clay for anything else either so I thought we should go out and get some – and that's exactly what we did. My mum took me to 'Hobby Craft' where we saw great big packs of different coloured modelling clay – it was awesome! Each colour was in a pack of its own and, better still, there was some flesh coloured clay – dead cool! I picked the colours I wanted and put them in the basket, but my mum had spotted a pretty box containing smaller amounts of various coloured clay. She wondered if

I'd like these instead. "No way," I said, "these are way better. It's a good job I'm here to stop you from just getting that small box. It doesn't even have flesh colour in it!" She replied something like, "OK Alex, we'll go with this clay. I'm pretty sure I wouldn't have got the small box anyway, I'd have thought you'd want the bigger one". We paid for the clay, packed it in bags, and took it home.

This time, as well as the animation, I decided to do a sort of tutorial type commentary on how I made them. As I was making the model, I recorded it on my webcam, explaining everything I was doing, to show people how to make models. When it was completed, I stopped recording, but I didn't go straight into the animation because, if Count Olaf were going to speak, he'd need ready planned words before I started animating him. So, using Microsoft Office Word, I wrote down what I wanted him to say and then started animating. I did another tutorial describing how to make the actual stop motion animation – I recorded it and kept explaining what I was doing and how to move the model and stuff like that. In the event I decided to stop recording before I had actually completed the film, otherwise I'd totally bore people watching it, because it took an incredibly long time to film an animation even if it was just a few seconds long. It was really, really, really hard work moving the lips – my hands were aching – but I was determined to complete it! However, I did go back and cut out some of Count Olaf's speech; even though the speech wasn't particularly long, it was ever such hard work, and I felt I needed to cut it down. At long last, I completed it, but... when I looked at the photos I saw with absolute dismay how many shadows there were! I just hadn't looked at the actual camera image, but I'd concentrated the whole time on moving the model and keeping out of the way when I took each shot. I wasn't pleased, but there was no way I was going to do all that hard work all over again. I'd just make sure I'd put a massive apology for it whenever I uploaded it to YouTube or my blog, or anywhere else. Anyway, I now decided to put it all together into a stop motion animation on my camera and then imported it to my computer, ready for the sound to be added. Using the sound recorder software on my computer, I began recording myself reading Count Olaf's speech. I had to repeat it over and over again, until I was confident – one single tongue twist and I'd stop recording and start again. I had to do it loads of times, but eventually I got it perfect (I think!). It was now ready to add to the animation. I imported both the animation and speech into 'Windows Movie Maker' and made sure the timing was alright – although it didn't actually fit perfectly. I still don't quite know how to do that – his speech went on for just a little bit longer than the animation. However, it was just the evil laugh at the end that went on longer, so I felt like it wasn't that bad for the film to turn black and then have Count Olaf's evil laugh. In fact, I thought it made it almost quite exciting and sinister. It kind of indicated that Olaf might still be there even when you can't see him. When I finished putting them together, I put the video on YouTube and it did get quite a lot of comments – despite the shadows, people liked it! Minus the shadows, I think it was the best animation I had done so far – I planned to keep doing more and more animations and I was pretty sure I wouldn't make the 'shadow' mistake again! Much to my surprise, a few people I've spoken to who have seen it, said they didn't even notice the shadows! That is seriously good to know. However, watching it recently, I don't think it was flawless, even if you take away the shadows. His lips are kind of all over the place. Anyway, unlike the other two animations I mentioned, I've managed to put this animation back onto YouTube on my new account, which you can find by looking up 'Count Olaf has a message to give to the world' on YouTube.[10]

*   *   *

One day, my grandma gave me a present. When I looked in the box, it was a set of Magnetix, which I thought was really cool. I decided I would use it to make another animation, so when I got home I started work on it, attaching and turning the Magnetix until I had made a cannon type model that shot out bullets. In my film, I had a dog (that was really a moneybox, in the form of a model dog) walk up to the cannon, which shot the dog dead. It turned out loads better than the Count Olaf film because it didn't have any shadows (even though my sister Alice was in the background a lot!). I decided not to use the animation option on my camera, but to complete the animation just by using 'Windows Movie Maker' (I now realized that when we had been considering getting the 'Stop Motion Pro' software, we could have simply used 'Windows Movie Maker' the entire time). After importing it to the computer, I edited it using Photo Plus, because I needed a bullet to come out of the cannon and shoot the dog, plus a flame when the bullet hit the dog. I used a picture of one of the balls that go in between each Magnetix for the bullet which I copied and pasted right next to the cannon.... making it a little nearer to the dog with each photo I took, before the dog eventually died. I used a picture of a flame and pasted that onto the dog, when he died, and then imported all of the photos into 'Windows Movie Maker'. It did look very like the dog had been shot by the bullet – this wouldn't have been successful if I'd used the animation option on my camera. I added music and uploaded it to YouTube. I think the bit when the bullet shot out stunned a few people because they wondered how I had done it! I was very pleased with it – it was the best one so far.

CHAPTER 16
I Start Wedding Photography (And Promptly Finish)

One day Donna told me she was getting married and asked, "Hey, Alex.... What do you think of having the important role of being the photographer at my wedding?" "Oh, yeah", I said, "That'd be good!" She said, "You don't have to if you don't want to, but we don't have a photographer, and we thought maybe we should give you this opportunity". I was pleased, but at the same time, pretty nervous. I knew I'd definitely need to practice, because I knew I'd find it very difficult to tell people where to stand, especially without anyone to prompt me. This would be partly because of nerves, and partly because I find it difficult to get people's attention. We'd have to go to the place where Donna's wedding was going to take place and practice taking loads of pictures.

Soon, after we found out about the wedding, my dad bought me a new lens. I really needed a lens with a much longer zoom if I was going to take photos of a wedding, so we got one, went outside and started using it. I took some pretty good photos with it, but it appeared to be suitable only for people, but not other things like landscapes or plants. I found out later that it did do other things as well, but you just had to change some kind of setting. This lens was pretty good, and I knew it'd be perfect for the wedding, so I began to practice for the big day!

One day we went to the church building where Donna was planning to get married. Before we went in, I practiced taking photos of Donna walking through the gate outside the church, and then we went in and I took photos of the pulpit and where the bride and groom would be standing when they were actually getting married. We also asked the people who were there in the building if they'd let me take a picture of them all and put them in the order I wanted. They agreed, so I took a picture or two of them.

The next day at the Horse Care Course we practiced again; taking pictures and telling people what I wanted them to do. I was a bit slow at explaining to them what I wanted because I really find getting people's attention extremely difficult. After this I knew that this part of the wedding wouldn't be easy. However, if I rehearsed, I hoped I'd do well, and perhaps I'd benefit from having done it – and in any case, it would be boring for me if I wasn't taking the photos!

I heard that originally Donna had considered not having a photographer. I definitely thought then (and still do think now) that if she's inviting someone to the wedding who's 'into' photography, she might as well use him to her advantage! So, we kept practicing more and more.

One day Donna, Esther, Alice and I went to where the reception was going to be held, so I could get to know the building and familiarise myself with being there and taking photos of everyone. The idea was that I should imagine what it would be like on the day, with all the guests standing around and me taking pictures of them. I was supposed to organise where Donna, Esther and Alice were to stand for photographs and things like that. I have to admit that I found it pretty difficult. I found imagining loads of people in the building that weren't there extremely difficult too. I sometimes find it hard to imagine things that aren't in front of me.

Well, soon it was the big day of the wedding! My family and I were there quite early. When we went into the church, the vicar asked me if I was the photographer. I said that I was and he told me a couple of things and then said something like, "Make sure you don't take any photos actually during the service". Everyone arrived and I was told to start taking photographs. The trouble was that I was pretty slow and often had to be reminded to organise people. At least I was only taking a few informal pictures at this point. After the ceremony I'd be doing it properly!

During the service I was just watching, but when Donna and her new husband went to sign the register, I was sent by my family to start taking pictures. I was really confused, in view of what the vicar had said about not taking photographs during the service, but my family seemed to be telling me to do just that! I whispered, "But that's not allowed!" One of them (I can't remember who) told me it was ok – so I went and took photos of the signing of the register.

When the ceremony was finished, I started taking photos. I didn't do much of the organization of the guests into groups – unfortunately it was Donna who did most of that. However, I did go around taking photos of all the things that were happening at the wedding. Even so, most of them I was told to take; I didn't do it automatically. People would just keep saying, "Take this! Take this! Take this! Take this!" When we got to the reception, I started to take more photos, but Donna told me to come forward and take pictures of people coming into the venue – I can't remember if I got every person who came through to line up for a photo, or if it was Donna, so I'll say it was Donna.

Anyway, I also told people where to stand and I did go around the church taking lots of informal photos of guests. Personally I prefer these, because they're more natural than the more formal ones. When the food was brought in, I took pictures of that and the top table. When it was time for the speeches, I took a couple of pictures from a distance, using the longer zoom lens, but when I looked at them, the quality was pretty bad – quite blurry and fuzzy.

When it was over and we had all gone home, my mum started telling everyone about my photography at Donna's wedding, and how well I had done – but I wasn't so pleased with how I'd done. I really didn't think I had spoken up enough. I'd been told to take a lot of the photographs, I hadn't managed to do it independently and naturally. Donna had been the one to get people's attention most of the time, not me – though, on the plus side, I had done a little bit of the organising, so it could have been a lot worse, but I felt it could have been a lot, lot better! However, my parents, Donna and most of the others seemed to think I really had done very well *and* Donna paid me for the work that I had done. I can't remember exactly how much, but it was a fairly decent amount!

I haven't referred to my Christian faith for a bit, so now I think this is a good opportunity to say something about where I was up to. I was (and still am) actually getting on quite well! I had become a member of the church, since now I was 16 I was old enough and I was finally able to go on Beach Mission! I had wanted to go for years, and now I was finally going with my sister, Naomi. I was very nervous – but that's normal for me (and I do know that pretty much anyone is nervous before starting something like that) – and yet excited too. I was worried that I wouldn't do very well at it, so Donna decided we should have a bit of practice. She suggested we should go to see the Beach Mission at Llandudno so that I could watch and see what they did, and try to imagine what it would be like being part of the team. We rehearsed a little bit at home as well, knowing that on Beach Mission I'd have to listen to instructions *very* carefully and maybe run a few things too. We knew it would be a challenge, but challenges are good! This was quite possibly one of the most challenging things I'd ever taken on – I was really nervous and frightened, but at least I was going to give it a try!

When it came to it, I actually quite enjoyed the experience. It was hard going and I made a couple of mistakes, which I hated and I didn't speak as much as I'd have liked, but overall it was well worth my going. One of the things you do when you're on Beach Mission is speak to complete strangers about the Christian faith. I found that very hard and I didn't really do it much, if at all, but it was the first time I'd ever been and I definitely wanted to go again the year after. I went in the summer of 2014. When I returned, I didn't go straight back to work, because I'd found Beach Mission so hard, I think I had a week off.

During this time, I was still making videos for YouTube on various aspects of autism and other subjects. Aunty Annette had watched some of them and, because of them, had gained a bit of an insight into the way I thought and felt. My mum found the same and, in addition, she saw how my videos had helped other people with autism and parents of autistic children. I think my mum and Aunty Annette had a talk and soon after Aunty Annette came into the room where I was and spoke a little bit about how helpful I had been in giving an insight into the difficulties that autism can bring. I don't remember exactly what she said, but I remember for definite her saying seven words, "I think you should write a book". I wasn't sure about it at first, but eventually she managed to convince me that it was a good idea. At first, Aunty Annette was the one typing, while I dictated to her what I wanted to write. I started off by speaking about my early childhood and how I used to find something as simple as going into a shop torture. I didn't like speaking about it at first, because I found it a bit embarrassing talking about how I found things. I also really didn't like other people reading it at first. Nevertheless, as I got going, I really enjoyed writing it. I thought that if it ever got published it would help parents. It was even a help to my mum and Aunty Annette and they knew me well. Anyway, I'm sure I don't need to tell you that the book I wrote is the very same one you're reading.

CHAPTER 17
Beginnings and Endings

I believe I haven't yet explained that I had started attending St John's Ambulance, which is a club similar to Scouts, where people learn different things, mainly focusing on medical information and first aid. At this point in time, the subject we were learning about was 'communication'. As she had done with Beavers, Cubs and Scouts, Donna went with me, although now managing to fade back her support to one of remaining in the background. The leader asked Donna to do a speech about her job working with young people who had autism, which was relevant to the topic of 'Communication' because autism often has an impact on a person's ability to communicate effectively. Donna told my mum and me about this request. She said that since I had spoken a lot about autism on YouTube she thought it would be a good idea for me to do the speech. I had mixed feelings about this. I couldn't decide if I should do it or not. All the young people from St. John's Ambulance would then know I had autism and, even at this point when I was 17, I was still pretty self-conscious about it, especially with young people. Yet I knew that if Donna went ahead and gave the speech everyone would still know that I had autism. I just didn't want them to know the truth of my condition. I also didn't really like the idea of making the speech myself because I was scared of speaking in front of people. I somehow didn't think I'd be able to do it.

However there was another part of me that thought, "I have this chance to tell all these young people about autism, and help them to understand what it's like to be autistic and if I got Donna to do the talk, it would feel like a wasted opportunity". I also thought that if I managed to do the speech I would have achieved something important. Deep down I think I knew this was something God wanted me to do.

I told Donna that I'd think about it. This was a decision I had to make, which was very difficult as a lot of the time I have to be in the situation to know what option is best. I struggled to come to a conclusion but eventually I decided to do it. I told Donna and she started to write down everything I wanted to say in my speech about autism, while I dictated it to her.

Soon after my mum got PowerPoint up on the computer and helped me make a presentation for the speech. I got some tips on public speaking from my sister Naomi who had done speeches before. Donna told the leader that I was going to do the speech and it was then planned.

I practiced many times every day for a couple of weeks beforehand, but I was still extremely nervous about doing it. The usual fears came into my head. I was worried that I would mess up and wouldn't be able to do the speech. I think Donna told me that if, on the day, I really couldn't manage it, and she would take over. In all honesty, that didn't make me feel any better, because if Donna took over, I would have felt afterwards like I had failed. That thought made me all the more determined to do this speech.

We decided that I'd also make the speech for the Riding for the Disabled Horse Care Course I attended. I'd first do it for the students there as a sort of practice round, and then I'd do it for St John's Ambulance. The day came when I was due to do the speech for the

Horse Care students. I was extremely nervous. In fact, I was pretty terrified! Just before I did it, I said to the students, "I'm really nervous about this." One of them replied, "Oh, there's no need to be nervous. You're among friends here." However, the truth is, if I know the audience, then that makes it all the more nerve-racking for me.

Anyway, I did the speech, and once I got going I did really well. The feedback I got from the students was extremely positive and some behaved as if they had met me for the first time, because I didn't speak much at Horse Care so they only knew me as being very quiet. One of the students was autistic himself, and couldn't speak very well. As he was watching it, I could tell he was taking it all in, and could relate to a lot of what I said.

Surely you are thinking that after this, I must have been confident for the speech at St. John's Ambulance. Right? Well, actually, no, I wasn't. I was just as nervous as ever about doing the talk. Firstly, I was nervous about telling them all about my autism, because I thought most of them didn't know I had autism. At the Horse Care Course, most of the students had a disability, so the audience there might as well know what mine was. In the case of St. John's Ambulance, I was with mainstream young people. I had known some of these young people for most of my life. I thought they might think less of me after I had explained all of my difficulties to them.

When I did the speech it went really well. I tried my hardest to control my anxiety. I managed to hide my nerves. My dad (who was there watching) didn't even realise I was nervous. I didn't get any questions though. They all seemed too surprised to ask anything and I don't blame them because I was also surprised. I never thought I'd be able to do one good speech, let alone two!

Meanwhile, Aunty Annette's husband, Uncle Steve had just got a new job down in the south of England, which was far way from where I lived, so Aunty Annette and her husband had to move away. Because of this, she could no longer work with me.

It was sad to know that she was going, but we didn't lose touch with her. I still write emails to her quite frequently, and she's one of the main editors of this book. On her last day we had one last banquet. The banquet we had was a McDonald's banquet. Donna also attended this banquet, since this was the last time Donna would see her for a while. It was the first and last banquet Donna attended. Donna didn't dress-up so we decided that she would come as a McDonald's customer. I dressed up as Ronald McDonald.

Now Aunty Annette had moved, my parents were thinking of getting one or two more people to work with me. Donna's husband, Tim, was asked to work with me as a life coach.

Aunty Annette had mainly helped me with academics, whereas Donna concentrated on independent living skills. Tim did activities with me such as snooker, going to the gym and boxing. However, he did do a touch of independent living skills as well. For example, when it came to playing snooker, he'd get me to ask for the snooker balls. I did enjoy doing these activities. I also found that he had similar interests to me, such as Star Wars and the Lord of the Rings, so he was a good person to talk to.

CHAPTER 18

'A' Factor As Opposed to the X-Factor

One day my mum told me that Autism Cymru (which is an organization for autism in Wales) was providing training for people with autism to become public speakers. She said that she'd get in touch with them about it. I was quite excited at the thought of being trained as a public speaker. My mum spoke by telephone to Lynn Plimley, the coordinator of the course, and arranged for us to meet her at a garden centre. My mum said that Lynn wanted me to write a presentation about my hopes for the future, just to show what my skills at writing presentations were like, so my mum helped me to create a PowerPoint presentation.

We met Lynn at the agreed place, where she looked at my 'Hopes for the Future' presentation on my laptop. She said she was impressed and told us about an event held at Theatre Clwyd where Collette Morgan (a well-known speaker with autism) was going to give the main talk. Lynn asked me if I would like to do a 10-minute speech about my hopes for the future before the main speaker did her speech. She also said I would get paid for doing this. I was up for this! I was nervous and really excited all at the same time! I agreed to do the speech.

During the next few weeks, I spent a lot of my time practicing the speech. My mum gave me a few ideas of what to say in the speech, but when I first started practicing, I struggled so much, pausing while speaking and talking negatively about my difficulties. My mum said I needed to make it funnier and more positive. I tried to take this on board. Each time I practiced, I'd record it on my webcam, watch it, and try to memorise the speech. It worked! I learnt the whole speech off by heart and used the PowerPoint slides as a reminder of what to say.

When the day arrived I was nervous as well as excited. I walked into the large Clwyd Room where I used to attend a drama group called Fuse. I think being familiar with the room helped. The room was full of big round tables with lots of people seated around them. I was allowed to bring my whole family and Donna; we are a big family and so had a whole table to ourselves. I was nervous, but I didn't give in to my nerves. Only a few years earlier in Fuse I had hid my face during one of the shows because I didn't want to be seen. I could easily have done something similar here. However, once I started to speak I found the nerves went and I quite enjoyed it, particularly when everybody clapped at the end. Apparently I didn't even come across as nervous and it went really well. This time, I got quite a lot of questions, which I thought was good.

Dad recorded the speech on my video camera and later, when I watched it, although I thought it was good, I felt there was room for improvement. A few of the jokes sounded too serious, and while the audience laughed at most of them, there were a couple of jokes at which they didn't laugh. For example, at one point when I was talking about being afraid of turning 18 (which was only a few weeks off) I said, "According to this test on the Internet, my mental age is 4 years old". I wasn't actually being serious - I was just joking and trying to make the audience laugh, but the problem was that I said it in such a serious voice that it sounded as if I was saying I really thought my mental age was that of a 4 year old. I did take this back straight afterwards and told them it was a joke, but no one seemed to be able to tell straight away, and when I watched it back later, I could see that I did sound serious. Although I'd meant to say it in quite a sarcastic voice, I failed miserably! Nitpicks aside, the speech did go very well considering I hadn't done many before and the audience certainly seemed impressed. Soon after, Autism Cymru sent me a cheque as payment for making the speech.

It wasn't long after this that Autism Cymru started training me in public speaking. However, there was a problem here, and that was that the people who were going to mentor me lived all the way down in South Wales. I lived in North Wales, which was too far for me to travel regularly, but the problem was solved through a Facebook group, called the 'A' Factor. It was agreed my mentors would train me through typing up comments and giving feedback using this group. I had three mentors: Lynn Plimley, Veronica Jones and Dean Beadle. Dean Beadle is a well-known public speaker who has Asperger Syndrome and does speeches about how Asperger affects him. I saw one of his speeches on YouTube and was really impressed by it! It was very funny, but also extremely positive about autism. If it is still on YouTube by the time you read this book, I recommend checking it out.

My first task was to post the speech I had done for Autism Cymru on the Facebook group. When I had done this, I was given feedback. They explained in what way I had done well, and how I could improve, which I think is always the best way to give feedback. I took their comments and suggestions on board. After the feedback for the 'Hopes for the Future' talk was dealt with, I was given the task of doing a presentation about 'What autism means to me'. I had nowhere to do this other than at my house. We wrote the presentation on PowerPoint, and then my mum filmed each slide and recorded me speaking about it separately. We did this because we wanted the mentors to be able to see the slide that related to that part of the talk. In truth, it was awkward, but it worked. When it came to posting this presentation on the Facebook group, my mentors said I had improved since the previous time and gave really positive feedback.

My dad arranged for me to give a presentation to the board members of the company for which he works. The next task my mentors at the 'A' Factor group had asked me to do was a speech about my early childhood with autism. We decided that it would make things easier if this was the speech I did at my dad's work. We could record me doing the live speech and use that recording to share on the Facebook group. This would mean I wouldn't have to be practicing two speeches at the same time. It would also make the recording better because it would be a video of me doing a speech in front of a live audience, rather than just in front of the videographer. When it came to doing this speech, I was especially nervous because I had only practiced for about a week. This even though it was a subject that I was quite confident with, because a lot of it was based on the first chapter of my book.

As I walked into the room I felt even more nervous. It was not a big room, and furthermore it was full of business people in suits sitting around one of the largest tables I have ever seen. They looked extremely serious and I felt very intimidated as they sat around the table watching me. I remember praying that God would help me to do the speech. I started doing the speech and managed to pull it off. I noticed I didn't get as many laughs as I had done previously with my 'Hopes for the Future' speech, and I felt like I had stumbled more than I should. When it was over, I did get extremely good feedback from the audience, but still I couldn't help but feel when I left the room that it hadn't gone very well. My parents said it had gone well and when I mentioned that I didn't get as many laughs as usual, they said, "You can't expect the same reaction from every audience. Audiences are all different".

When I came to post the video on the Facebook group, I was quite anxious and worried that my mentors would be disappointed and feel as though I taken a few steps backwards, so I apologized for it not being as good. However, I found out that not only were they impressed, but they also said it was the best one I had done so far! I was very surprised and relieved to read this.

Soon after, Lynn Plimley told me about an event being held at Glyndŵr University for young people with autism to attend. The event was called 'Exploring opportunities after school'. She said that the 'A' Factor would be there, and she also invited me to do a speech. For this one she said to take all the slides from my previous presentations that I thought were the most important and put them together to make a 30-minute presentation. She also said that I would get paid to do this speech.

We also came across a free website. It wasn't a very fancy one, but better than nothing. On this website, we explained that I did Public speaking, trying to increase people's understanding and raise awareness of autism spectrum conditions, and told them how to get in touch if they wanted me to speak for their organisation. We also designed business cards from Vista-print. They were dark brown, which made it hard to read the black print clearly, but nevertheless I felt really pleased to have my own business cards. We also got a banner designed from Vista-Print. My brother's fiancée Suzanne (who is a graphic designer) created some posters for us to give to people. We tried creating posters but struggled, so Suzanne provided the solution – she did it for free too, which was very kind. We also created a Facebook page about my Public speaking. By doing all of this, I hoped to get well known.

When it came to the big event at Glyndŵr, I brought the business cards, the banner, and some of my photos for people to see. When I got there, I saw quite a few displays of autistic people's art. I met one guy who had studied animation at Glyndŵr University whose artwork was displayed. He showed my mum his entire artwork file. There was another autistic person who was interested in pirates and had a display of pirate cartoon work. I enjoyed looking at this artwork and felt reminded that so many people with autism have amazing gifts.

I finally met Dean Beadle in person. I already felt as though I knew him through the 'A' Factor group. I was inspired to see someone with autism doing as well as Dean Beadle. Suddenly I had met fellow autistic people who were succeeding in life. Maybe I could succeed too! I also met with Lynn Plimley, but my other mentor Veronica Jones couldn't make it that day. I met another boy called Robert Parton who was mentored through the 'A' Factor. He made a really good speech. I was scheduled to do the speech twice. The first time I did it, I was in front of high school children with autism. They really responded well and asked a lot of questions. The second speech was in front of adults, and once again they responded well, although I thought the first speech went better, because I was rather tired when it came to the second one. Near to the end of the day I saw Dean Beadle's speech, and it was very funny!

When it had finished, I thought, "Overall, it was a very good day, and I'm glad I went". Soon after, I read the feedback sheets to all the speakers of the day and it was all very positive.

Not long after this event, a cheque was sent to me for the talk I did.

CHAPTER 19
Business as Usual (And the Saga of the Rings)

My training was now complete and I am very thankful to all three people at the 'A' Factor group for their support and encouragement. I had improved in public speaking tremendously since I had started, and was now getting more and more opportunities to speak for different organisations, including the Clwyd Special Riding Centre, the Welsh Assembly, the National Autistic Society and many more. At this point in time, it was a hobby – and, generally I wasn't being paid. A lot of the time, normally just after I had done a speech, a member of the audience would ask what my fee was and I'd tell them that I did it for free (although my parents and I were starting to think about charging a fee).

During this time, my brother Ben was engaged to be married and he asked me to be a Best Man at his wedding; I was one of two that he had. If you've been to many weddings then you will know that a Best Man does a speech about the groom, and I was honoured to be given this role. For years, I had anticipated this day would come and, though I wanted to do it, I feared I would not be capable. However, as by this point I had some experience with public speaking, I was hopeful. However, the Best Man had other tasks in addition to making a speech, but since I wasn't the only Best Man, I didn't have to shoulder the responsibility alone - just some of it! I knew, though, that I would definitely need to practice for this role. I'd not only need to practice the speech, but whatever other jobs I'd be given.

My parents made sure we had a list of things I needed to do from relatively early on in the preparations, so that I could memorise what needed doing. As usual, I was nervous, but I was, at the same time, excited. One of the jobs I was given was that of ring-bearer - in other words I'd be responsible for the rings until I was meant to give them to Ben and Suzanne. I was also asked to announce when the bride and groom and their respective parents were ready to be seated at the top table at the reception afterwards... and obviously, I was given the task of making a speech about Ben.

Now, the main problem was that while I had done speeches, they had all been about autism, which is a subject I know a lot about - this one would be about something quite different. The question was, would I be able to pull off this speech as well? Well, I wasn't sure, but I was willing to try.

When I began working on the speech, I was struggling to come up with things to say about Ben, but thankfully I did still manage to come up with some pretty funny stories about him. As usual, I did have support from my mum. I used PowerPoint for the speech, though whether I'd have the use of a projector wasn't certain at this point. However, I still used that with which I was familiar, even if I'd have to print the PowerPoint slides off as a reminder for my key points. My mum thought I should use the projector, but I disagreed because you don't usually see that at weddings, and I'm someone who likes things to be done the way they normally are. I still wasn't sure at this point though.

Anyway, after a few weeks of practicing, it was finally the big day! I was very nervous, my brother had trusted me and I didn't want to let him down. I was worried that I'd mess up! I was frightened that perhaps I'd lose the rings, or do something that would make me look like an idiot. This made me all the more determined. When it was time for me to give the rings, I accidentally dropped them. This didn't particularly embarrass me. All I had been worried about was losing them. I dropped them, but so what? Everyone can drop things. I was maybe slightly embarrassed, but not very, until shortly after Esther said something that was not very encouraging. She said, "You dropped the rings?" In a voice indicating that was one of the worst mistakes known to man. I said, "Well, yeah. What's so bad about that? Sometimes people do drop things". She said, "But still, you dropped the rings!" I was like thinking, "Thanks Esther! You've just made my anxiety worse." Naa... I'm just kidding (kind of). She didn't mean to make it worse. Later on, I found out that she was just surprised she hadn't noticed. A while after, I told Tim (Donna's husband) that I had dropped the rings and I think he said he hadn't noticed, and I know he said he had been to weddings where that had happened, so that certainly made me feel better!

When it came to announcing the bride, groom and parents to the table, I was having technical difficulties with the microphone, which was a bit awkward, but they were soon resolved. I managed well, and when I had finished, I was relieved that I didn't mess up, but it wasn't over yet. I had a speech to do after dinner. When Ben announced for me to do the speech, I was like, "This is it!" I stood up and began speaking. Once I got going, I was doing pretty well, and was getting a lot of laughs! When the speeches were over, I had people coming up to me every few seconds to compliment me on my speech. They all really enjoyed it! Even the following Sunday, the people at the Church were still talking about my speech. You're probably thinking "Ok... We get it! Your speech was good. Stop boasting!" But I'm just making the point that, despite worrying that I'd never be able to do it, I did it and did it well, so let me say to anyone who has to do a speech for something: if you work hard enough to do the speech, it may not be as hard as you think. Not long after this, Naomi got married to Aunty Annette's son (the one who was good at computers who I briefly mentioned in this book). Naomi married him and I was an Usher at this wedding. I'm not going to go into as much detail about this, because I didn't have to do a speech and I don't want to bore you with too much 'wedding talk'!

About six months later, Suzanne (Ben's wife) started working on a new website for me. This wasn't something we asked her to do, she just volunteered for free. The website I used was kind of tacky, and un-interesting, so I was grateful for the idea that Suzanne was going to create me a new one. She was not only going to create a new website, but new business cards and posters as well.[11] Our old posters were actually out of date, because they said I was 18, and by now I was 19 and had been doing Public speaking for over a year. She also created a logo for me to use for everything to do with my business. The logo had the words, "Alex Lowery speaks about autism". Each word was a different colour.

Suzanne and Ben also gave my parents (who were supporting me with the business) and me some tips. At this point, the speeches I had done for the 'A' Factor group were still public on YouTube. Ben and Suzanne thought this wasn't good, because we wanted people to get interested in booking me to speak, and if they had already seen my speeches on YouTube, they might think there's no point. So they suggested creating a new video for YouTube containing small extracts of several of my speeches, to give a taster of what I do, to get people interested and wanting to see more. I liked this idea!

Soon after, I started working on it, editing bits of each speech together into one video. When it was finished, I uploaded it to YouTube, but then soon after my mum suggested that I should create a new YouTube channel just for videos about autism, which could be like my business channel. The channel I already owned had autism videos, but it also had other things like animations, film reviews and a maths comedy I created as part of an Open University course I did. I soon created a new channel just for autism videos, and started adding more videos about autism to the channel. I added some that I had already done, and I also created a few more. I created one about my day-to-day struggles with anxiety. I've still got this channel, and I hope to continue adding videos to it.

When Suzanne finished working on my website, I looked at it and I thought it was fantastic! It was extremely professional. It did not disappoint me!

My parents had thought about how much work I put into my speeches and had finally come up with a fee for me, although for some audiences the fee might be different. We weren't planning on charging until the beginning of August because that's when my education would finish. This would also mean that Donna and Tim would stop being paid to work with me.

My mum took me to meet a lady who helped people with their businesses. My mum showed her all the business cards and posters that Suzanne had designed and I think she was impressed. My mum and this lady were talking for a while about my business but most of what was said I didn't really understand. A lot of it was about money and that kind of thing. At the end of the meeting, this lady told us about an event being held at the Old Town Hall, called the Dragons' Den Cymru. I had never heard of the Dragons' Den Cymru, but apparently Dragons' Den is a TV series featuring people displaying their business ideas in order to secure investment finance from a panel of business people. The Dragons' Den in Holywell wasn't going on the television (kind of to my disappointment), and it wasn't for investment but rather for mentorship. Anyway, a similar thing to what happens in the TV show was going to happen in the Old Town Hall.

My mum said I had to do a mini-presentation about my business for the Dragons' Den. After a lot of work and practising, I was ready to do this presentation.

Finally we were going into the Old Town Hall for the Dragons' Den, and I saw quite a few people with different business ideas there. I had my photo taken next to my business stuff. Finally, when I went in to see the Dragons (which are the people of the Dragons' Den), I saw several people sitting down in a room watching me and welcoming me in. I set up the laptop and performed this mini-presentation. All the dragons were very impressed with both my business and what I had performed.

They asked me quite a few questions - some I found difficult, and others I found easy.

One lady in particular by the name of Margaret Carter was very inspired by what I was doing, and seemed very interested. She had her own business at Patchwork Pâté Food Company. She gave me her business card. After talking for a while, my mum and I left the building, both feeling encouraged by the feedback we had received from these professional business people.

Soon after, my mum received an email from Margaret Carter saying that she'd like to mentor me in my business. In other words, she wanted to give my mum and me advice in running the business. It was agreed that we'd meet her again in the Old Town Hall.

When we saw her, she spoke to us about different things concerning the business. So far, my mum had been the one to contact organisations to ask if they'd like me to speak. She did this because I find it very difficult to talk to people on the phone. However, Margaret thought I should be the one to phone people up and tell them about myself, explaining that if I were to speak on the phone, they would be more likely to want me. She asked me what things I wanted to achieve through my business and said that when I got home I should make a list of all the things and put a date by them, this would show when I hoped they would be completed. I thought it was a good idea for me to phone people up, but I was very scared to do it all the same. The following week my mum and Donna started working with me making phone calls. We'd have a lot of practise beforehand, imagining different scenarios until eventually I'd do the real thing. When I first began making phone calls it was really difficult. I spoke too quickly and would not give the person at the other end of the phone time to take in what I was saying. Margaret had asked me to write a script. I did this, but I found it difficult to follow on the phone.

As I got going with phoning people, I did start to do better, but it was still difficult. My mum's actually still working on phone calls with me and she actually still makes a lot of the phone calls for me. It takes me all afternoon just to make a few, but I want to keep on trying to improve. My mum says it's just anxiety and the more I do the better I will get. When I phoned people up, some were interested, others were not. I phoned up Donna's doctor's surgery, and they said they would like me to do a talk. I was glad to help medical people understand autism more.

Not long after, I met with Margaret again, but this time I was with Donna. One of the tasks Margaret asked me to do in our last meeting was to write a list of all the ways I'd like to earn money. In our second meeting, I showed the list I had made to Margaret, and she gave me feedback. This time Donna was taking notes. I tried to take notes as well, but I just couldn't. I could not take notes and listen at the same time. It was just too much for me! For the next few months, I was still getting help from Margaret and still am. I was getting more opportunities to speak.

It was also coming very close to when Donna and Tim would finish working with me. Donna said even though she's no longer paid, she'd still do a few things for me, like take me to the vaulting team, drive me to speeches and go with me to the Horse Care Course, but she wouldn't be doing all that she had previously. Tim also said that I could still do some things with him sometimes.

To say good-bye to Donna, we all went out with her to a Chinese restaurant. Donna has worked with me for longer than anyone else, except my parents, but it's not like I'm not seeing her again. My mum registered me as self-employed. I was now officially in business. I was working for myself with support from my parents.

This is my life's story until now. I had worried for a long time that I would never get a job and would never live independently. I still don't live independently, but I have now got a job. It feels like I've accomplished an ambition. Of course, I still can't say what the future will hold for my business or me, but all I can say is there is hope. I'm still hoping to continue learning new life skills. I also hope that I'll be able to live independently. I still worry about my future, but the fact is that I've achieved so much so far that I can't say what the future will hold. One thing that's certain is that my autism will never be cured. I'll have it for the rest of my life, but I still hope to continue making progress and get as much out of life as possible, even though there may be many barriers in the way. I still have a very supportive family, and God has helped me in more ways than the greatest maths genius could count.

I am very thankful to Donna, Aunty Annette and all the others who have worked with me over the years. I'm also thankful to my parents but most of all the Lord God for all the help I've received. If it wasn't for all the support I've had, I may even be screaming in shops to this day.

Well, thank you for reading my story. I hope you enjoyed it and I hope you've learned a lot from it.

Appendix 1

Below is the story of Patrick the Big Bad creepy Monster that I was hoping to make into a film, which to this day I still haven't done in the way I originally wanted.

Scene 1: Patrick, a human child, receives a book of wisdom from his father, who also tells him never to go to the Land of the Dead Wasp....but Patrick is tempted to go and satisfy his curiosity.

Scene 2: Patrick finally gives into temptation about 10 years later and goes to the Land of the Dead Wasp. As soon as he gets there, he regrets it. It's a horrible place with no way out. Suddenly, a giant wasp appears and stings him. It was agony, a pain worse than anything Patrick had ever experienced. He then begins to change physically – extra arms grow; his teeth become sharp, like a shark's; he emerges like an enormous spider. He regretted what he'd done, but there was no going back for Patrick.

Scene 3: Enter the Hishnocks (ugly people who lived in the Land of the Dead Wasp) to make Patrick their king – who was very pleased at this turn of events. Patrick and his evil Hishnock followers plotted to return to the old world, using the wasp that had stung Patrick. They plotted to take revenge by attacking everyone at a railway station, so Patrick gave orders to his troops and the bombardment began. Patrick began stinging people and there were tanks on which sat little black dogs firing guns – but one man (William) and his dog (Dylan) saved the day. I can't quite remember how because I've since lost the last part of the script, but as Patrick is defeated, he shrinks, his hair turns white and he collapses on the floor as if he's had an electric shock. Everyone

---

hails William as a hero and he becomes very wealthy. Patrick and the Hishnocks go to prison, growing old and even uglier.

Scene 4: Patrick reads the book of wisdom his father had given him so long ago. He reads about the Saviour of the world; that we are all sinners; that God loves us so much that He sent His Son to die for us; and, finally, that all those that trust in Him shall be saved. Patrick sits in prison and weeps, praying for forgiveness. He becomes a Christian and although he's still an ugly monster (albeit smaller!) on the outside, he now had a clean heart and began to speak to the other prisoners about the gospel, warning them never to go to the Land of the Dead Wasp.

THE END

I hope you enjoyed the story; I haven't recorded every tiny detail, but it just gives the broad outline. I now see lots of stuff that are a little forced and could be better. For example, when Patrick first got to the Land of the Dead Wasp, the script says that there was no going back to the old world, but yet he ends up doing just that by flying on a giant wasp, and what I now think is that he should have done that in the first place! It's one big plot hole, but another thing that doesn't make sense is why exactly Patrick wanted to take revenge. In the old world he was good and it was kind of like, 'Now, I've got these powers, I'll kill everyone!' without any good reason. If I were ever to re-write the story, I'd certainly improve it and fix the plot holes and inconsistencies.

Notes

1. A Film on how I found the world when I was younger. 'Perception and attention with autism'. The URL is here: https://www.youtube.com/watch?v=MoJwzSaxMu8

2. Homeschooling a child with autism by Sylvia Lowery see here: http://www.alexlowery.co.uk/autism-and-home-education

3. Alex's views of ABA therapy can be watched here: https://www.youtube.com/watch?v=aN5N8hIBTgM

4. A film about autism and flexibility of thought which uses an original story Alex wrote as a child is here: https://www.youtube.com/watch?v=Iul5gT0UBNk

5. You can hear Alex talk about his experience of learning he had autism with his DVD 'Growing up with Autism' which is available to purchase here: http://www.alexlowery.co.uk/talks-training/training-dvds/

6. Alex has worked on two films about Stimming with Fixers.org.uk:

   6.1. Fixers Stimming story on ITV which can be viewed here: https://www.youtube.com/watch?v=P8RC1OxlrJY

   6.2. 'Stimming a social guidance video' which can be viewed here: https://www.youtube.com/watch?v=S-65WzrYNbw

7. An article by Alex 'Why Stimming is a big part of my life' can be viewed here: http://www.alexlowery.co.uk/why-stimming-is-a-big-part-of-my-life-and-why-it-should-never-be-stopped/

8. Here is a blog post which has the original photos of the clay models: http://busyatthemoment.blogspot.co.uk/2006/05/anination-characters-i-like-these.html

9. Here is a link to some of Alex's photos: http://alexisdoingphotography.blogspot.com/

10. Here is one of the original animations that Alex made, 'Count Olaf has a message to give to the world': https://www.youtube.com/watch?v=o5sd72fyyP8

11. Alex's business website can be viewed here: http://www.alexlowery.co.uk/